THE
MARSHALL CAVENDISH
ILLUSTRATED ENCYCLOPEDIA
OF
DISCOVERY
AND
EXPLORATION

The death of Genghis Khan.

THE
MARSHALL CAVENDISH
ILLUSTRATED ENCYCLOPEDIA
OF
DISCOVERY
AND
EXPLORATION

VOLUME 2

BEYOND THE HORIZON
Malcolm Ross MacDonald

EDITORIAL COORDINATION
Beppie Harrison, John Mason
REVISION EDITOR
Donna Wood

Marshall Cavendish

New York   ·   London   ·   Toronto   ·   Sydney

Reference Edition Published 1990
© Marshall Cavendish Limited 1990
© J G Ferguson Publishing Company/Aldus Books Ltd. 1971

Published by Marshall Cavendish Corporation
147 West Merrick Road, Freeport, Long Island, NY 11520

Printed by Mladinska knjiga, jugoslavija
Bound in Italy by L.E.G.O. S.p.A., Vicenza

Library of Congress Cataloging-in-Publication Data
Discovery and exploration.
   Summary: Describes the journeys of the world's explorers from the first men who traveled beyond the then-known world to the scientific explorations of today.
   ISBN 1-85435-114-1
   1. Discoveries (in geography) – Juvenile literature.
[1. Discoveries (in geography)   2. Explorers.]
G175, D57 1990
910'. 9 – dc20   89-15723
                                                                         CIP
                                                                         AC

   ISBN 1-85435-121-4   Beyond the Horizon

Introduction

The dramatic saga of Man's exploration of his world; his courage and endurance against all odds, is expertly told in the seventeen volumes of the *Discovery and Exploration* encyclopedia.

The exploits of the first intrepid adventurers from Phoenicia, Greece and Rome on their perilous journeys into the unknown, exploration in the Dark Ages which ventured west to the Atlantic and across Asia to China, and the charting of the vast Pacific, a huge area of bleak, unyielding ocean from which many ships did not return, shows the determination of these early explorers in their search for even greater knowledge of the world about them.

Covered in these volumes are the oldest trades routes toward the spice and treasure of the Orient and the merchants who discovered them, the ruthless Conquistadors who put their thirst for gold above all else and the pioneering trappers and traders who were responsible for opening up North America. The motives of many of these men may have been purely mercenary, but we still owe them the debt of their discoveries, the roots of which still exist in customs and practices in many parts of the modern world to this day.

Painstakingly researched and minute in detail, these volumes of *Discovery and Exploration* contain a record of almost every important geographical discovery to take place in the history of mankind. Highly illustrated with a wealth of ancient documents, contemporary paintings, maps and illuminating extracts from the explorers' personal accounts of their journeys, these books make fascinating reading and are visually exciting; quite different from the dry works of reference that many of us are used to.

These are real adventure stories, telling of the explorers who broke through the barriers of their time regardless of personal hardship.

The later volumes move on in time to the great discoveries of the 17th, 18th and 19th centuries: the colonization and exploration of Australia and New Zealand, the taming of the Sahara and the unique challenge represented by Africa and Asia, lands of savagery and suffering to the often ill-prepared explorers of bygone days.

Some relatively recent exploration work occupies the final volumes of the set; the journeys to the North and South Poles, undersea exploration by pioneers like Jacques Cousteau, the endeavors of some famous mountaineers and, lastly, a history of man's foray into space and his achievements there. An 80 page Index volume completes the set.

Contents

**VOLUME 2
BEYOND THE HORIZON**

A detail from the Catalan Atlas of 1375, showing the brothers Polo traveling by camel caravan.

The Chinese not only invented paper, but were the first nation to use paper currency. Here the khan is seen supervising the distribution of paper money.

The Great Atlantic Ocean

1

Above: a stone carving of Saint Patrick, patron saint of Ireland. He spent most of his life converting the Irish to the Christian faith.

Left: in this world map of the A.D. 900's Britain (Brittannia) and Ireland (Hibernia) appear at bottom left, while the Scandinavian lands are shown as islands separate from Europe.

More than 400 years after the birth of Christ, the European world still centered on the Mediterranean Sea. To the west, the European horizon was bounded by the Atlantic Ocean, a great mass of water stretching away into the unknown. To the east lay the vast lands of Asia with their fierce barbarian inhabitants. The peoples of Europe feared what might lie in these distant regions, and were content to stay within the world they knew. Few had dared to cross the horizon. When, in the A.D. 400's, the Europeans did eventually break down the barrier of fear which had prevented them from venturing into the unknown, it was the Atlantic Ocean that they first explored. Eight hundred more years were to pass before they turned their attention to the East.

In the A.D. 400's, the peoples living on the fringes of the Atlantic Ocean had no idea of what might lie farther to the west. Ancient classical writers had described mysterious and beautiful lands called the "Fortunate Islands" or "Islands of the Blessed" a long way out into the Atlantic. These islands have since been associated with the Azores, the Canaries, or even the West Indies. But, at that time, no European is known to have sailed beyond the Madeira Islands. No one knew of the existence of America, nor even of Iceland and Greenland much nearer home. As far as the people of Europe were concerned, the vast sea might stretch for ever.

The fears and superstitions that hedged around the lives of Europeans of the time made exploration difficult. People thought that the world might be flat, and that, if they sailed too far west, they would fall off the edge. Moreover, they believed that the sea was the home of fierce monsters, and that its waters were ruled by powerful gods. Sailors were able to set a rough course at sea by the stars, but there were no proper navigational instruments, and certainly no charts. The first steps toward discovering the secrets of the Atlantic were taken by two peoples of northern Europe, and for very different reasons. The Irish braved the ocean to convert to Christianity any pagans that they might find. The Viking peoples of Scandinavia, on the other hand, regarded it simply as the route to rich countries where they could raid, or settle.

The Irish and the Vikings were not the first people to sail the waters of the Atlantic. The fishermen of western Europe and the British Isles had long been familiar with the coastal waters. And as long ago as 1100 B.C., mariners from Phoenicia—a country in the eastern Mediterranean on the coasts of present-day Syria, Lebanon, and Israel—had sailed through the Pillars of Hercules (the Strait of Gibraltar) into the Atlantic. By the 400's B.C., Phoenician sailors from the colony of Carthage, according to ancient writers, reached the British Isles in search of tin. Greek sailors, too, braved the vast ocean. In about 325 B.C., Pytheas, a Greek explorer from Massalia (present-day Marseille), sailed past England and Scotland and possibly beyond the Shetland Islands. However, mariners still did not dare to venture far out of sight of land. Seamen driven out to sea by storms seldom survived, and the few sailors lucky enough to find their way back could tell only of vast, empty waters. The Europeans believed that Europe's western shores were the ultimate edge of civilization. They thought that nothing of value could lie beyond.

It was the religious activity of the Irish that was responsible for filling in the first blank spaces on the map of the Atlantic. For more than 400 years, Irish monks sailed their frail boats over its perilous waters in their efforts to find new, isolated lands suitable for the hermit way of life. They also made many converts to Christianity in the British Isles. Even more important, for the first time they broke beyond the confines of the European world.

Before the 400's, Ireland had been almost entirely pagan. It was a land of scattered homesteads and small individual communities

Above: hermit cells at the Skelligs, County Kerry, Ireland. Irish hermits seeking solitude were among the first people to travel in frail boats across the unknown North Atlantic.
Left: a page from the Book of Kells. Probably produced by the Irish monks of Kells in the 700's or 800's, this illuminated copy of the Gospels is a fine example of early Christian art.

Right: the Irish abbot Saint Brendan with his companions aboard ship on one of his voyages. The book describing his travels tells how his rudderless boat, steered by one oar and with one sail, was encircled by a huge fish with its tail in its mouth.

under the rule of local noblemen. Most of the population lived by fishing, or near-subsistence farming, or by raiding the property of neighbors more wealthy than themselves. Early in the 400's, one such raiding party returned from the west coast of Britain carrying among its booty a 16-year-old boy called Patrick, who had been captured as a slave. Patrick was later to become the patron saint of Ireland. After six years in captivity, Patrick escaped and fled to France, where he became a monk. In 432, he returned to Ireland and spent the rest of his life on missionary tours throughout the country. In some places he converted the pagan inhabitants to Christianity. In others he organized the tiny pockets of Christianity which already existed, and brought Ireland in closer touch with Rome and the church of western Europe.

In Patrick's time there were no cities, nor large towns, and the country was divided into many small principalities. This feature of Ireland in the 400's aided the establishment of monasteries throughout the country. The noblemen converted by Patrick, or by other wandering priests, set up local monasteries, each independent of the others. Into these monasteries they gathered their relations and lay followers—that is, those followers who were not members of the clergy. When a monastery throve, it followed the example set by Patrick and sent out missionary groups in its turn. Many of the missionaries traveled long distances within Ireland itself. Many made much longer journeys far beyond the Irish shores.

The Irish brand of Christianity was a passionate one, and Irish Christians were particularly zealous in doing what they considered to be their duty. Armed with this zeal, the Irish set out to convert their neighbors. Among their first converts were other people of Celtic origin like themselves. They established communities in southwest England, in Cornwall, where the Romans had introduced Christianity centuries earlier. They also turned their attention to the

Welsh, who had also known Christianity. The Irish established Christian foundations in France and Germany, and as far away as northern Italy. Many of these monasteries kept records from which we derive much of our knowledge of the earliest Irish travelers overseas.

In 563, Saint Columba, a monk from the north of Ireland, established a monastery on Iona, a tiny island off the west coast of what is now Scotland. From Iona, monks began the conversion of the Pictish people on the mainland. Iona rapidly became the early center of the church in Scotland, and served to keep the Irishmen who came to settle the country in touch with their homeland.

From the 500's onward, Irish monks and hermits began to turn their attention away from the known world. Sometimes alone, sometimes accompanied by experienced sailors and supporting lay communities, they traveled and settled in little-known lands. The earliest travelers sailed in *coracles*, the simple boats used by all Celtic

Above: sheep grazing on the Faeroes, a group of islands in the North Atlantic Ocean. The Irish-Scots were the first people to reach the Faeroes, but their settlements there lasted only 100 years. When the first Norsemen arrived, they found only sheep.

Right: Norsemen on the Faeroes *flensing* (stripping blubber from) a whale. Even in those days, whaling was an important commercial activity. The Norsemen traveled to the Faeroes, then pushed on to Iceland and Greenland.

peoples of the time. Coracles had wicker frames covered with cowhide. Normally they were shaped like broad, round-bottomed, keelless bowls. Although frail, the coracles had important advantages. They were unlikely to sink because they were light, rode with the waves, and did not easily ship water or capsize. Coracles could be rowed or, if the wind were in the right direction, sailed. Coracle-making has been preserved as a craft in Ireland and in Wales, and coracles are still used by some Irish and Welsh fishermen. Today, however, the frames are of wood and the covering of canvas or tarred cloth. Nowadays only very small coracles are built, but in Columba's time they were large enough to transport men, goods, and livestock.

Individual Irish hermits and small bands of holy men seem to have treated sea-voyaging as a pious venture. They saw it as their own version of the sojourn in desert and wilderness through which Jesus and the early saints sought closer communion with God. In the process they traveled farther and farther from home.

Most of the stories about the exploits of the first brave voyagers have survived only in legends. In these tales, ancient Celtic heroes and later Christian heroes are confused, and mythology conflicts with fact. Some of the stories, however, do have a firm basis of fact, as we know from existing historical records. The most famous of these stories concerns Saint Brendan, one of the first generation of

missionaries, and, according to the legend, one of the first Irishmen to travel beyond the shores of Europe to the islands of the Atlantic.

Saint Brendan (484–577) was an Irish abbot born at the Bay of Tralee, in the southwestern part of Ireland. Brendan became a monk. Determined to live the life of a hermit, he is reported to have sailed out into the Atlantic in search of solitude. Among the places he visited were the Sheep Islands—perhaps identifiable with the modern Faeroes, a group of islands in the North Atlantic Ocean north of the Shetlands—and the Paradise of Birds—perhaps the Shetlands or Outer Hebrides. He also reached what he thought were the Islands of the Blessed described by the ancient classical writers. Many of the stories of Brendan's activities carry a strong moral and allegorical content, but there is enough sober description in them to convince us that they tell of real voyages rather than imaginary ones. We know from records kept in monasteries that Brendan certainly visited Scotland and Wales.

The Irish-Scots, too, began to travel beyond the confines of their own land. It is a matter of historical fact that they reached the Faeroes in about 700. In about 825, an Irish monk named Dicuil, who studied and taught in Europe, wrote an account of his country-men's colony in the Faeroes in a work called *Concerning the Dimensions of the World*. He wrote: "There are many other islands to the north of Britain which can be reached from the northernmost isles by sailing directly for two days and nights under full sail with a favorable wind. A religious man told me he sailed to them in quite a small boat. Some of the islands are fairly small; most are separated by narrow straits. Hermits from out [of] Scotia [Scotland] had lived there for about a hundred years, but they have now abandoned the place

Below: the southeast coast of Iceland, with black sand caused by volcanic ash and lava erosion. Most of the early explorers and settlers landed on this coast, the first convenient landfall from the Faeroes or on the long sea voyage from Scandinavia.

to the Norse brigands. Only their sheep remain. We have never found mention of these islands in the books of other authors.'' The fact that this is the first record of a colony settled 125 years previously shows the loose structure of Irish Christianity then.

From the Faeroes, it was only two days' sailing to the southeastern waters of Iceland. The way lay across the uncharted seas of the North Atlantic but this cannot have deterred the Irish-Scots for we know that, in about 770, they arrived in Iceland. In the same book in which he mentions the Faeroes, Dicuil also says that he had heard

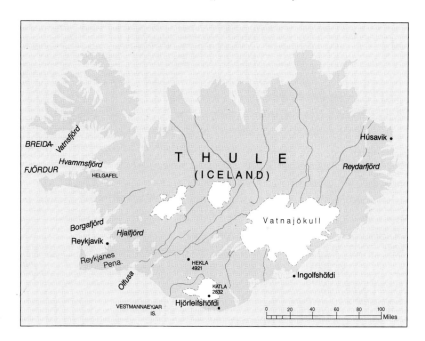

Above right: Irish monks probably first reached Iceland, which they called Thule, in about 770. About a century later, Viking raiders first rediscovered and then settled this island of harsh contrasts. The map shows their most important settlements.

of Irish monks reaching Iceland, which he refers to as Thyle or Thule. "It is now 30 years since certain priests who had been on that island [Iceland] from the first of February to the first of August, told that not only at the time of the summer solstice [midsummer] but also before and after, the setting sun hides as it might be hidden by a small mound, so that there is not even the shortest period of darkness. It is so light that a man could even pick lice out of a shirt, just as though the sun were up. And had they been on a high mountain perhaps the sun would have been visible all night.

"At the season of greatest cold they always had alternation of day and night, except around the winter solstice. But at a day's sail northward they found the sea frozen."

From other sources, it is clear that in Dicuil's time Irish monks were regularly traveling to and from the Iceland communities, probably using the Faeroes as a station on the way.

During the 700's, the people who were to continue the Irish explorations of the North Atlantic first appeared on the European scene. They were the Vikings, sometimes called the Norsemen—the men from the north. Sweeping down from the harsh countries of Scandinavia, the Norsemen made for the fertile lands of Europe,

Left: a print showing the midnight sun in Iceland, from a book by Olaus Magnus, a Swedish author of the 1500's. In Iceland, as in other far northern lands, it is light all night at certain times of the year. Here, the mountains glow in the sun, as the stars shine above.

where they burned and looted, taking gold, cattle, and slaves. In 795, they reached Ireland. Soon the Norsemen began to raid farther afield. By way of the Hebrides and the Faeroes they eventually reached Iceland. It was these Norse raiders who were responsible for driving the Irish of Iceland away, possibly farther west.

The descendants of the early Norsemen mention in their writings the Irish of Iceland: "Christians lived here [Reykjavík] whom the Norsemen call 'papar.' Later they went away because they did not wish to live here together with heathen men. They left behind Irish books, bells, and crosiers [ceremonial staves carried by bishops]." It is probably something of an understatement for the writer of this description to say that the Irish left simply because they "did not wish to live with heathen men." By the 870's, the Irish at home and abroad had experienced nearly a century of Norse ferocity. It is much more likely that the little band of Irishmen had sighted the Norse ships and had left in a hurry, abandoning all their possessions.

As Norsemen had reached Iceland via the Faeroes and Hebrides, the Iceland Irish probably judged it unwise to make for home through those same waters. They had heard how the Norsemen treated the inhabitants of lands they wanted to settle. The Irish had been in Iceland long enough not just to have sailed around it, but also to have learned of the larger island of Greenland, two days' to the west. They may have arrived in Greenland by about 870. When Norsemen were known to be approaching Iceland, the route westward was probably the safest way out for the Irish settlers. This conjectured voyage from Iceland to Greenland was possibly the first crossing of the North Atlantic by European sailors.

The Norse writings contain indirect evidence of the Irish occupation of Greenland. Sometime in the 980's, for instance, some storm-driven Norsemen, forced to winter on the Greenland coast, fell to squabbling over a purse of Celtic gold they found in a burial mound. And on his first reconnaissance of Greenland in 982, Eric the Red found deserted houses and boats similar to the coracles used by the Irish.

There is a theory, not yet fully substantiated, that the Irish may have been the first Europeans to reach the shores of North America. Norse writings contain tales of white Christian men in a land called either Hvitramannaland or Ireland the Great. The stories, often highly fanciful in detail, refer quite casually to Norsemen,

Right: a beautifully carved crosier (bishop's stave) from Lismore, a town in Ireland sacked by the Norsemen. The ritual objects which the Irish left in Iceland, when they were driven out by the ferocious Norsemen, included things such as crosiers.

blown off course on their way to Greenland, having reached a country where white men "went about in white robes, carrying poles and banners and singing loudly." They mention this with no further explanation, as though it were common knowledge.

The earliest French missionaries to Canada in the 1500's and 1600's, came across rites which could just possibly have been the last vestiges of Irish Christianity. In their efforts to convert the Iroquois (Indians of the locality), the French often encountered strange and perverted reminiscences of Christian ritual quite out

of character with other aspects of Iroquois religion. Crosses were widely used in tattoos and craft decorations. During a week of festivities a dog was crucified. Except that it took place in winter not spring, the ceremony in many ways resembled the Christian Holy Week.

As yet, however, no concrete evidence has been found to prove that the Irish missionaries really did reach North America. Stories of their settlement of the country are still based only on speculation, and nothing has been proved beyond reasonable doubt.

Left: a modern Greenland landscape—the village of Kap Dan, Kulusuk Island, on the east coast. This is one of the islands reached by the Vikings, and possibly the Irish as well, on their voyages to the west from Iceland.

Below: a drawing of a North American Indian holding a strip of *wampum* (beadwork) decorated with small crosses. Such designs have led scholars to believe that the Christian Irish may have reached North America before the Vikings set foot there.

Post tauis igitur magni celuda sed
p constituta é qua fabule poetari intastari
mi nerua que primu ea excogitasse
muium fuerat hominib: praui
habet autem stellas inpupe
mo mali in subcari na

stellaru ordinem nduis
collocata dicunt ppr
dicit et maire qd antea
nduali ingenio fecisse
ui inlatere .v. insum
.v. sunt .xvii.

Arcturis adlam luda serpens plabitur argo.
Conuerans ipse portans cumlumine puppim.
Hon alie naues ut inalto pondere proras
X nte solent rostro neptunio prata secantes
S edconuera retro caeli se ploca portat

The Viking Raiders

2

The Irish went to far-distant lands in order to come closer to God through solitude. Theirs was a religious motive. The next group of travelers, the Vikings, ventured abroad for quite different reasons. They migrated not for pious reasons, nor yet to trade, but to plunder, wage war, and win themselves first glory and later land.

The Vikings came from the north, from the modern Scandinavian countries of Norway, Sweden, and Denmark. In the old Norse language, the word *Viking* described a man who came from a *fiord*— an inlet or a creek. To go *i viking* came to mean to leave one's inlet home and go raiding and marauding. A Viking, therefore, came to mean, particularly to the peoples of other parts of Europe, a ferocious merciless pirate.

The plundering raids of the Vikings were not just the whim and pleasure of a blood-loving race. They were a solution to many problems in the Viking homelands. In the so-called Dark Ages, overpopulation and land shortage were extreme in Scandinavia. The limitations of farming around the fiords of the Atlantic coastline, with its scant soil and cold winter weather, were severe. At first, the Vikings sowed crops before setting out on their raids, and returned later to harvest them. As time passed, however, periods of violent internal dispute in Denmark and long family power struggles in the many small kingdoms in Norway, forced numbers of dispossessed Norsemen to look elsewhere for a living. Forced into exile by hunger or by new overlords, the Vikings took to the seas. Fortunately for those who wanted, or were compelled, to get away, the Viking ships were the best-developed sailing vessels of their time. They were to remain so for several centuries. Viking warships became a familiar and hated sight to the inhabitants of the European countries to the south, east, and west of Scandinavia. They prayed for storms and rough seas, and welcomed harsh winters when the raiders could not travel far. "From the fury of the Northmen, good Lord deliver us!" was a frequent prayer among the frightened people along the coasts of northern Europe.

The prospect of a violent end in some skirmish in a foreign land was no deterrent to the Vikings. Death in battle was to them the most glorious end to life on earth. Odin, chief of the gods they believed in, particularly admired valor in fighting. He knew of everything that happened on earth, and in time of battle sent warlike goddesses, known as Valkyries, to collect dead heroes from the

Above: a painting from an Icelandic manuscript, depicting Valhalla, (in Norse mythology the hall of slain warriors). On the left is the great palace, with 540 doors, each so wide that 800 warriors could pass through side by side. On the right is the serpent of Midgard (Middle Earth, the home of mankind), which lay coiled around the world. The god Thor tried unsuccessfully to capture the serpent with an ox's head as bait.

battlefield to transport them to the heavenly Valhalla, the hall of dead heroes. There the warriors fought again each day outside the heavenly palace, those who were killed in the fighting being later restored to life. Afterward, they feasted and drank wine. Before wounded human warriors died in battle, they chanted the record of their past victories and moments of bravery so that Odin, reminded of how valiant they had been, would send his Valkyries for them.

The success of the Viking attacks on other peoples depended to a large extent on the element of surprise. The swiftness of their ships and their ability to come close inshore or penetrate shallow rivers made this possible. The warships used by the Vikings for making sudden raids on their neighbors' lands were called long ships, from their long, narrow shape. The Vikings' victims came to know the boats as dragon ships because they often had a fearsome dragon's head carved on the prow. The long ships were very fast but not

always very seaworthy, and they often broke their backs in rough weather. They had oars, sometimes a square sail as well, carried between 30 and 40 oarsmen, and could achieve impressive speeds.

The ships used by Vikings for longer voyages were bigger and much more solidly built, but still long and narrow. Like the long ships, they were made of wooden slats, usually of oak, joined by roundheaded iron rivets and caulked with tarred animal hair or wool. Oars were of pine wood and varied in length along the ship's side so that they struck the water together. The mast was also of pine, with a square woolen sail. The larger ships frequently had a small ship's boat stored on board or towed behind.

The Vikings launched their first attack on their neighbors, the inhabitants of the British Isles, in the A.D. 780's. At the time the British Isles were subdivided into many kingdoms that were constantly at war with one another. England was made up of

Above: the Oseberg ship dates from around A.D. 800, and was found, well-preserved in clay, more than a thousand years later. Together with the Gokstad ship, unearthed some years earlier, it is the most important surviving example of a Viking long ship. *Clinker-built* (with overlapping planks riveted or lashed together), and carrying a single square sail, with up to 10 rows of oars on either side, it was probably used as a ceremonial ship.

three major kingdoms—Northumbria, Mercia, and Wessex—and four smaller kingdoms—East Anglia, Essex, Kent, and Sussex. Scotland was divided into Dalriada, Strathclyde, and the kingdom of the Picts, but, by the mid-700's, the Picts had become the most powerful of these kingdoms. In Ireland, the High King in Tara was paid homage by the leaders of a number of small kingdoms. Wales was similarly partitioned.

In 789, three Viking ships landed on the coast of Dorset in southwest England. The invaders killed the local chief, collected booty,

Left: in 875, the monks fled from Lindisfarne, in fear of a second Viking attack. They took with them the famous Lindisfarne Gospels, now in the British Museum. Later, monks did return to the island, and these ruins date from the 1100's and 1200's.

Right: a fanciful medieval painting of a fleet of Viking ships on its way to invade England. The Danes stepped up their attacks in the 800's, and some settled permanently in England.

and then returned to their homeland. Four years later, the rich monastery on Lindisfarne, also called Holy Island, off Northumbria in the north of England, was sacked and burned. "In this year terrible portents appeared over Northumbria and sadly affrighted the inhabitants; these were exceptional flashes of lightning, and fiery dragons were seen flying in the air. A great famine followed soon upon these signs, and a little after that in the same year . . . the harrying of the heathen miserably destroyed God's church in Lindisfarne by rapine and slaughter." For some years thereafter, the Vikings were busy raiding Ireland.

In the 830's, they again resumed their attacks on England. It became necessary for a permanent watch to be kept along the coasts of England for Viking ships ready for the attack. When they were sighted on the horizon, church bells would be tolled, men would hurry to arms, and priests would rush to bury their treasure. At first, the Vikings were content to attack, pick up as much booty as they could carry, and retreat to their ships. But in 851, they changed

their tactics and wintered on the Isle of Thanet in Kent.

A few years later, the Vikings felt strong and practiced enough in warfare to conquer England. In 867, a strong force of Vikings set up a base in York. By the 870's, they had defeated the armies of East Anglia and Northumbria and had forced the neighboring kingdom of Mercia to pay tribute. Then Alfred, king of Wessex, defeated the attacking Danes, who suffered so many casualties that they at length agreed to a truce. In 878, the Danes, led by Guthrum, overran Wessex but were finally routed at the Battle of Edington in Wiltshire. Guthrum had no choice but to make peace, and in 886, agreed to a pact dividing England between himself and Alfred. Land in the north and east came under the rule of the Danes, the *Danelaw* as it was called.

Another wave of Viking invasions began in 980, when Vikings raided the east and south coasts. The English king of the time, a feeble-hearted man, was known as Ethelred the Unready. Instead of leading his people into battle, he tried to buy the enemy off with gold. The tax he collected from his people for the purpose was known as *Danegeld* (Dane gold). The Vikings returned again and again to collect their easy winnings. In 1013, a king of Denmark named Sweyn Forkbeard invaded England, but died before its conquest was complete. The final conquest was completed by his son Canute, who was crowned King of England in 1016.

Scotland also suffered at the hands of the Vikings. The blow first fell on the islands of the Orkneys, Shetlands, and Hebrides. In 795, Vikings pillaged the island of Iona, and in the 800's, they began raiding the mainland. A great host stormed Dumbarton, capital of Strathclyde, in 870. In 904, they ravaged Dunkeld, farther to the east. The Scottish king eventually regained the Hebrides some

Above: King Canute placing a cross on an altar. Canute was king of Denmark and Norway and ruled England for 19 years, after the death of Ethelred's son Edmund Ironside.

Left: the Danes took home valuable plunder from their raids. The Gundestrup bowl, believed to have been made by Celtic craftsmen, was probably taken in northern France. The base of the bowl shows a hunting scene, with dogs attacking a bull and the hunter poised to kill it with a sword.

hundreds of years later in 1266. The Orkneys and Shetlands, how-ever, remained under Scandinavian rule until the 1470's.

The first raid on Ireland took place in 795, when the monastery on Lambay Island, off the eastern Irish coast north of Dublin, was sacked. The people of Ireland did not wear armor and were easy victims for the Vikings, who carried two-edged swords, iron axes, and daggers. To protect themselves, the Vikings carried round, hide-covered wooden shields with iron bosses. Chieftains wore corselets of iron rings, other Vikings had corselets of leather or thick cloth. Some wore round or conical helmets.

A fleet from Norway arrived in 832 and captured Armagh, the center of the Irish church. In 841, the Vikings founded Dublin and established bases at Wexford, Cork and Limerick. "The sea spewed forth floods of foreigners over Erin [Ireland] so that no haven, no landing place, no stronghold, no fort, no castle might be found, but it was submerged by waves of Vikings and pirates." During the late 900's, Norsemen settled along the south coast of Wales.

As far as the rest of Europe was concerned during this period,

Above: the coronation in A.D. 800, of Charles the Great (Charlemagne) as Emperor of the Romans. Viking attacks during Charlemagne's life-time were thrown back, but after his death the empire was disrupted and the raiders' task was much easier.

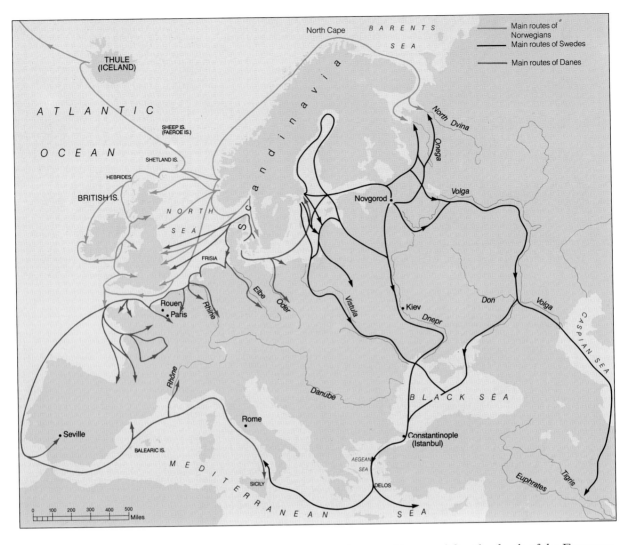

Above: the Vikings from Scandinavia traveled far and wide in their long ships between the 700's and the 1100's. Their main routes for raiding and later for settlement were across the North Sea to the British Isles, and across the Atlantic to Iceland and later to Greenland. Some Danish Vikings, however, raided the Atlantic coast of Europe and, passing through the Strait of Gibraltar, attacked the Mediterranean coasts of Spain, France, and Italy. Vikings from Sweden sailed and rowed many hundreds of miles along the rivers Volga, Dnepr, and Vistula to raid as far south as the eastern Mediterranean and even the Tigris Valley.

the Vikings were causing equal havoc. After the death of the Emperor Charlemagne in 814 and the disintegration of his vast empire, western Europe was in a state of great unrest. The large areas of France, Germany, and northern Italy which had been united under the emperor were now divided out among squabbling leaders. The countries were obviously weak and vulnerable, and this gave the Vikings a chance to attack and subdue individual nations.

The Danes invaded Frisia (the northern part of The Netherlands) in 834. In 864, they diverted the course of the Rhine River and thereby caused the decline of the important trading town of Dorestadt, which was on the river. Rouen in France was sacked in 841. Vikings entered Paris on Easter Sunday in 845, and sacked the city. The Frankish king paid 700 pounds of silver to persuade them to depart peacefully. The French kings tried many times to buy the Vikings off with Danegeld, but this only brought more Vikings eager for such easy spoils.

In the 800's, a Viking group invaded northern France. In 911, the French king bribed their leader by granting him a large slice of land which became Normandy—the land of the Norsemen. It was a descendant of the Vikings of Normandy, William the Conqueror, who defeated Harold of England at the Battle of Hastings in 1066.

During this time, Spain was ruled by the Moors. When Vikings raided Seville in 844, they took on more than they had bargained for. The well-disciplined Moslems finally routed the rough Norsemen and forced them to return most of the booty. The Moorish leader, the emir, sent 200 severed Viking heads to his allies in Tangier, in northern Africa, as evidence of his triumph.

But the Vikings were determined men and were not easily put off. Sixty-two ships under Bjorn Ironside and Hastein sailed from Brittany for Spain in 859. When Moslem forces proved too strong, the Vikings gave up and instead raided the north African coasts in the region of Cap des Trois Fourches, on the north coast of what is now Morocco. The warriors continued by way of the Balearic Islands to islands at the mouth of the Rhône River, where they spent the winter. In the spring of 860, they sailed south along the Italian coast with the intention of capturing Rome. Arriving at a magnificent city on the coast, which they imagined to be Rome, the Vikings tricked the inhabitants into allowing them into the city. There they found, to their dismay, that they had captured the little, relatively unimportant, seaport of Luna.

While the Danes and Norwegians were pillaging western Europe, Swedish Vikings were making raids on Russia. The Slavs and Finns who then lived there came to look on the Swedes as protectors and paid them tribute. The Varangians, one of the tribes of Swedish Vikings, were called *Rus* by the Finns, and some experts think this is how Russia got its name.

The Rus were more successful in trade than the Danish and Norwegian Vikings were. In 862, their chieftain Rurik arrived in Novgorod, north of Lake Ilmen, and established a center of commerce there. Rurik was succeeded by Oleg who, in 882, captured the city of Kiev on the Dnepr River. He also fortified the surrounding towns against the Khazars of the south and the savage Patzinaks who lived at the mouth of the Volga River. Merchants from Novgorod sailed down the Msta and the Volga rivers to the Caspian Sea, where they exchanged slaves and furs for silver. From Kiev they sailed down

Above: a woodcut from the book by Olaus Magnus, showing Rus Vikings carrying a boat overland on a trading mission. The Rus were traders as well as warriors, and they took furs, skins, honey, and other goods to sell to the inhabitants of the land which became known as Russia.

Right: the Rus were not welcomed peacefully everywhere. Here a group of Byzantine (Middle Eastern) cavalrymen are overwhelming some Vikings.

the Dnepr River to the Black Sea and Constantinople (now Istanbul), then capital of the Byzantine Empire. Early in the 900's, they approached Constantinople, and the Byzantine emperor made a trade agreement with them. Often the Patzinaks would try to ambush the convoy of boats as they came down the river. This was made possible because, at places where there were rapids or sandbanks, the boats had to be carried or hauled overland.

In 914, 16 Rus ships sailed down the Volga, through the territory of the Khazars, and ravaged the Persian coast of the Caspian Sea. At the mouth of the Volga they were defeated. The very few survivors were finally exterminated by the Khazars. In 941, another Rus expedition tried to capture Constantinople, but failed. On a voyage across the Aegean Sea, a band of Rus may have made a journey to the sacred island of Delos. The proof of their visit is a rhyme, carved in their script on a stone lion.

One Viking who was not interested in killing and booty was Ottar of Norway, a merchant shipowner who traded with the Finns for bearskins, walrus tusks, and hides. Ottar sailed north along the coast of Norway until he reached North Cape, the northernmost point of Europe. He then followed the coast around, first to the east, and then to the south, until he reached the mouth of a river. This was probably the North Dvina, or the Onega, in northern Russia. Ottar was the first European to round North Cape and sail through

Left: this stone lion, which sits outside the Royal Arsenal in Venice, was taken from the Greek port of Piraeus and may have originated on the island of Delos. The Swedish runic inscription carved on its flanks and legs suggests that the Vikings may have sailed as far south as the Aegean.

the Barents Sea, which lies north of Norway and European Russia. His voyage took place 700 years before the sea was entered by the Dutch navigator Willem Barents.

It was commonly believed that the Dark Ages (A.D. 400's to 900's) get their name because during that time learning died out in Europe. However, we now know that monks, particularly the Irish, were fine scholars. Even so, relatively little is known about what was happening in the world during this time, so how do we know what the Vikings did and where they went?

Three main sources of information are available. Sometimes they support one another, sometimes they provide apparently conflicting pieces of evidence. The first source is the wealth of archaeological remains dating from Viking times. For centuries, and as a result of ever-improving modern techniques, particularly in the last century, professional and amateur archaeologists have been discovering Viking ruins, tools, and weapons all over Europe and beyond. Often their finds confirm, or put into perspective, details of the picture of Viking activity we get from two other principal sources. These are the Norse sagas (prose narratives) of the 1100's–1300's, and the contemporary accounts of historians and chroniclers of the countries the Vikings invaded.

Scholars hold conflicting views about the origin of the Norse sagas. Some now think that they are the result of a conscious effort at storytelling, rather than simply legends passed by word of mouth from generation to generation and then written down.

Above: North Cape, a promontory near the northernmost tip of Norway. The Viking merchant Ottar sailed around this island on his epic voyage around northern Norway to the Barents Sea and the White Sea. Ottar gave a firsthand account of his voyage to King Alfred of England.

The latter theory is, however, still current. During the Viking age there were no books or other ready-made pastimes for the long, dark winter evenings. The sagas probably began as tales of heroism and adventure told around the fireside and handed down from father to son. Repetition by word of mouth is a notoriously bad means for the accurate transmission of information. And good storytellers, then as now, prefer not to be too closely restricted to the facts. Inevitably, with the passing of time, stories which were originally true were changed and romanticized to make them more exciting.

Above: a page from *Eric the Red's Saga*. This folio tells the story of how and why Eric named the new-found country of Greenland.

Left: an Icelandic painting of a colonist's family gathered to listen to the reading of a saga—a story describing the voyages and adventures of the early Norse heroes.

Some tales must doubtless have been lost for ever, and with them individual heroes and their journeys. But during the classical age of saga writing, the 1200's, about 120 sagas and many short stories were written down. The most important sources of our knowledge are the *Landnamabók*, first written down in the 1200's, and the *Flateyjarbók*, a collection of sagas written down by two priests between 1387 and 1394. From this material, scholars have been able to piece together what would otherwise have been a very confused period of history.

Iceland and Greenland

3

In the 800's, despite the booty they were carrying back to Scandinavia from raids on the British Isles and the rest of Europe, the Vikings' needs constantly outstripped the meager resources of their fiordlands. Instead of depending on short marauding voyages, they began to look for places where they might settle permanently.

During the period between 860 and 870, three Viking voyagers are believed to have reached the country known today as Iceland. It is possible, however, that there were earlier, unrecorded voyages.

According to one version of the *Landnamabók*, the first landfall was made, purely accidentally, by a Swede called Gardar Svarsson. He sailed from his home in Scandinavia to claim a family inheritance in the Hebrides, but was driven off course by a fearful storm which swept him northwest across the Atlantic to the southeastern coast of Iceland. In calmer weather, Gardar sailed north and spent the winter at Húsavik—house bay. Continuing around Iceland the following summer, he proved beyond doubt that it was an island. Gardar named the island Gardarsholm, after himself. On his return home he praised it very highly, making it sound an appealing alternative to Scandinavia.

In another version of the *Landnamabók*, Naddod, a Norwegian, is said to have discovered Iceland. He too was storm-tossed across the sea, and landed at Reydarfjord in the Austfirthir. In the hope of seeing signs of human habitation, Naddod climbed a mountain, Reydarfjall, but could see no evidence that people lived on the island. As he and his men sailed for home, a heavy snowstorm enveloped the land behind them, and so Naddod named it Snaeland—land of snow.

The first Viking to go to Iceland with the intention of settling there was a Norwegian called Floki Vilgerdasson. Taking his family and livestock with him, Floki offered up sacrifices to the gods and set sail. His party stopped off at the Shetlands and the Faeroes, and then made for Iceland. When they were well on their way, Floki set free one of three ravens he had taken with him. The raven flew straight back to the land they had left. Some time later, Floki released a second raven. This one flew up into the air and then returned

Left: the lava-covered landscape near Thingvellir in Iceland. Thingvellir was the site of the *Althing* (Icelandic national assembly), for over 800 years. It is today preserved as a place of special historic interest.

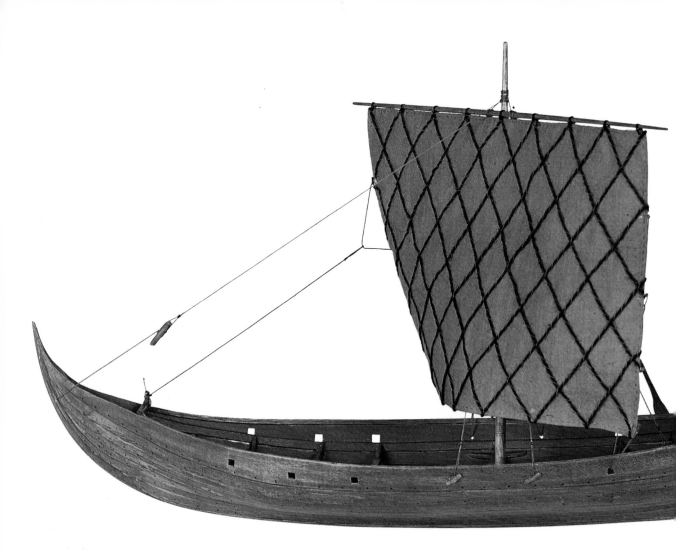

and perched on the rigging, so he knew they were still many miles from land. Then Floki loosed the third raven. It flew on ahead and gave him a bearing for land.

The ship sailed along the south coast of Iceland and then north to Breidhafjördhur, where the company stopped at a place called Vatnsfjord. They found its waters full of fish, and it was because they spent so much time fishing and sailing that they failed to make provision for winter. When the cold weather set in, the livestock perished for lack of hay.

In the spring, Floki climbed a mountain from which he could see the pack ice in the fiords, and so he called the land Iceland. After their experience of winter conditions, the settlers thought the land too hard for living in and prepared to sail home. Because of high winds, the ship failed to clear the Reykjanes Peninsula and was forced to turn back. Floki and his family therefore had to spend the following winter at Borgafjord. When he eventually got back to Norway, Floki, now nicknamed Raven Floki, had nothing good to say of his adventures. But a companion, Herjolf, not wishing, we are

Right: a modern view of Húsavik (house bay), on the north coast of Iceland. This is the place where the Swede Gardar spent the winter during his round tour of the island.

Above: a scale model of a small merchant ship, like those which plied between the Baltic and the North Sea. Smaller than the long ships, but also propelled by oars and a single sail, this type of vessel was used for ocean travel, and, more important, to carry cargo.

Right: a print illustrating Vikings with harpoons hunting seals on ice floes. Seals have always been hunted for fur, oil, and blubber.

told, either to condemn or to condone Iceland, "spoke well of some things and ill of others." A second, named Thorolf, was very enthusiastic about the country he had visited and told avid listeners of his adventures.

Around 870, two foster brothers, Ingólfur Arnason and Leif Hrodmarsson, were forced to give up their land in Norway after being involved in some vicious killings. A drunken young man had sworn that he would marry Ingólfur's sister and no other woman. Because Ingólfur's sister was already betrothed to Leif, this vow cost the young man his life. Within a year the young man's brother had also been killed. Forced to flee the country, Ingólfur and Leif decided to go to see the land Raven Floki talked about. They fitted out a big ship, probably in this case not a warship but a *knärr*. (A knärr was a merchant ship in common use at the time, longer and broader in the beam than a warship.) They explored the Alptafjord area of Austfirthir. After wintering in Iceland, they went home, planning to return to settle in the land they thought so promising.

The country they had chosen to colonize was one of harsh contrasts. Only the land around the coast was fertile and habitable. The interior of Iceland consists of deserts of lava—the molten rock that

Right: peasants threshing corn, from an Anglo-Saxon manuscript. Before his second voyage to Iceland, Leif Hrodmarsson made a raiding expedition to Ireland, where he captured 10 such peasants and took them back to Iceland to work as thralls (slaves).

pours out of volcanoes—and glaciers. Iceland lies in the North Atlantic Ocean and its northernmost point nearly touches the Arctic Circle. An eighth of it is covered with glaciers. Iceland is set across the Mid-Atlantic Ridge, a great fault in the earth's crust which runs from Jan Mayen Island in the Arctic through Iceland, the Azores, Tristan da Cunha, and on southward. Because of the volcanic activity along this fault, Iceland is constructed largely of volcanic material. Many volcanoes, notably Hekla and Katla, have erupted

Right: Iceland's interior contains many volcanoes, some of which were active when the Vikings arrived.
This woodcut of the 1500's includes the most famous, Mount Hekla. Mount Hekla has erupted on many occasions.

many times since the country was first occupied. Volcanoes occasionally erupt underneath the glaciers. In various places all over Iceland the earth's crust is very thin, and hot springs are found.

Ingólfur and Leif did not have time to discover or realize all these disadvantages before they returned to Norway full of enthusiasm for this new land. Ingólfur stayed to raise money and to interest people in going with him to Iceland. Leif went off on another Viking expedition to Ireland to capture booty and slaves. During this visit, Leif became known as Hjörleif or Sword Leif. He got this name because he is supposed to have entered an underground house or chamber which became filled with light from a sword held in a man's hand. He killed the man and, taking the sword and other riches, continued to plunder far and wide in Ireland. Taking back 10 thralls (slaves) he rejoined his foster brother in Norway.

Three or four years after their first voyage to Iceland, probably around 874, the two men were ready to sail back. Each had a ship and took his family, retainers, and slaves with him. On sighting the coast of Iceland, Ingólfur cast overboard the high-seat pillars (ornately carved poles) from his homestead in Norway. These were richly carved with sacred images and dedicated to the god Thor. Ingólfur vowed that wherever they drifted ashore, there he would make his home. In the meantime, as winter was drawing near, he spent the cold months at a place still called Ingolfshofdi, on the south coast below Vatnajökull.

Hjörleif traveled another 60 miles west and landed at Mýrdals-sandr, a coastal stretch of marsh and sand. He built two great houses at a site known as Hjörleifshofdi.

In the spring, Hjörleif decided to sow corn. Having only one ox, he also hitched his thralls to the plow. While Hjörleif was in his house, one of the Irish thralls suggested to the other that they should kill the ox and say that a bear had slain it. Presumably, neither they nor Hjörleif knew that there are no bears in Iceland. As Hjörleif and his men scattered in search of the bear, the thralls attacked and killed them. Then the thralls collected all the small belongings, seized the women, stole one of the boats, and made their way to some islands to the southwest of Iceland.

Meanwhile, Ingólfur had sent two of his thralls westward along the shore to look for his pillars. When they came to Hjörleifshofdi and saw what had happened, they returned to Ingólfur and told him about it. Ingólfur sought out the killers, slew them, and reclaimed the women. He then returned to Hjörleifshofdi, where his party spent the second winter. The islands the thralls had fled to became known as Vestmannaeyjar—the isles of the west men, which is what the Vikings called the Irish.

Ingólfur's third winter in Iceland was spent on the Olfusa River, and it was during this time that he found his high-seat pillars again. He settled there and called the place Reykjavík (smoky bay) because of the steam from the hot springs in the area. Ingólfur's party settled in the land between the Olfusa River and Hjalfjord, north of

Above: in 1963, an undersea volcano started to erupt south of the Vest-mannaeyjar. Its eruption formed a new island, which is called Surtsey.

Reykjavík—the first permanent community in Iceland. Later they came to be revered in Icelandic lore as Iceland's founding fathers.

During the late 800's, Harold Fairhair became Norway's first king. Norway had previously been divided into districts governed by *jarls* (petty chiefs). Harold was a local chieftain who warred against the jarls both on the land and from the sea. He vowed he would not cut his hair or bathe until he had conquered all his enemies. When at last he trimmed his hair and washed it, having presumably achieved his aim, his followers were amazed at his appearance and gave him the name Fairhair.

Many once-powerful men whose lands Harold usurped, saw him as a tyrant and fled the country. Iceland now became an obvious place of refuge, and "there began a great emigration out of Norway until Harold placed a ban upon it because he feared that the country would be abandoned."

Breidhafjördhur, where Floki had landed, was settled by a man called Thorolf Mostrarskogg. On Helgafel (holy mountain) he built a temple dedicated to Thor, and the mountain was made sacred, a place where no harm should befall man or beast.

Aud, the Deep Minded, widow of a Viking killed in battle in Ireland shortly after he had proclaimed himself king of Dublin, settled around Hvammsfjord at the head of Breidhafjördhur. Her son Thorstein made his home in the Hebrides, and her grand-daughters founded a noble lineage on the Faeroe Islands. Being a baptized Christian, Aud set up crosses and an altar on her land. When she died, however, her followers reverted to paganism and made sacrifices on her altar.

The early pioneers found good grazing for their cattle and also grew a modest supply of grain. Lakes and rivers were full of trout and salmon and the seas were rich in herring and seal. Sometimes whales were washed ashore, providing the islanders with food and

Right: a silver amulet, in the shape of a cross but with a monster's head, found in southern Iceland. The first Viking settlers in Iceland were pagans, but in the year 1000, the Althing decreed that Christianity should be the new state religion.

oil. Eider ducks and many other types of birds bred on the island.

We know from the sagas that within 60 years of its discovery, by the 930's, Iceland was fully occupied. The *Landnamabók* notes the names of 400 families, the elite of the settlers, many of whom had been Vikings or were of noble blood. Roughly one-seventh of the settlers had Irish origins or connections. The majority came from southwest Norway, the others by way of Scotland, the Orkneys, the Shetlands, and the Faeroes.

The Iceland communities took their law, language, and religion from Norway. Some of the settlers were already Christians, but to begin with others were less committed to Christianity. For example, Helgi the Lean "believed in Christ, and yet made vows to Thor for sea-voyages and in tight corners, for everything which struck him as of real importance!" By the early 1000's, Iceland was officially Christian under the jurisdiction of the pope.

After Iceland had been fully colonized, its new inhabitants turned increasingly toward the land and settled down to become farmers. But, as in Scandinavia, the amount of fertile farmland was insufficient for the number of people who wanted to live there. By 976, most of the best land had been claimed and only infertile land awaited new-comers. That year also saw a great famine in Iceland which dis-illusioned many of its inhabitants.

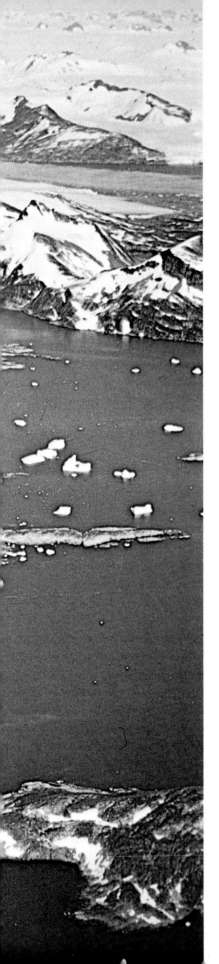

Left: an aerial view of the east coast of Greenland. This was the type of bleak scenery sighted by the first Vikings from Iceland. These settlers continued southward and set up their first bases on the more fertile and friendly western coast.

Right: Eric the Red, rather fancifully depicted by an artist of the 1600's. He is wearing medieval armor belonging to a period some 500 years later than his own. Eric and his companions were the first Vikings to explore the coast of Greenland and later to settle there.

Some 75 years earlier, around 900, reports of land farther to the west began to filter back to the Vikings in Iceland. At that time, a Viking named Gunnbjørn was driven off course while sailing from Norway to Iceland. Blown to the west, he saw a new, bleak and rocky coast. Gunnbjørn made no attempt to land, but when he eventually arrived in Iceland he made it known that he had seen new territory. As a result of the famine and lack of unclaimed fertile land, Icelanders began to think seriously about moving west.

The first of the Norsemen, so far as is known, to do anything more than talk about the unknown land, was a young settler named Eric the Red. Eric had come to Iceland with his father, who had been exiled from Norway for killing a man. In 982, Eric was outlawed from Iceland for a period of three years as the result of a serious feud. He determined to concentrate on looking for Gunnbjørn's land in the unexplored west.

Eric set off with a band of followers in 982. The company sailed west. After only a few days they sighted land. The country looked barren and uninviting, so Eric and his men turned south. Soon, they rounded a cape, and found that the land turned north. The travelers found this coast more pleasant than the one where they had first landed, and decided to pass the winter there. They called the place where they wintered Eriksey—Eric's island—in the entrance to Eriksfjord. With the arrival of spring, Eric and his men started up the coast again, naming many places on their way. They returned to the south for the second winter, and made another reconnaissance

Above: the eider duck is one of the numerous arctic and subarctic sea birds. Even in Viking times, the fluffy plumage—eider down—was an important commodity, and the birds were afforded special protection.

trip the following summer. After spending yet another winter in Eriksfjord, the party finally returned to Iceland, their period of banishment over.

Back in Iceland, Eric talked at length and with great enthusiasm of the land he had spent the last three years exploring. Then, becoming involved in new quarrels with old enemies, he decided finally to sail back to his new land and colonize it. Eric called his discovery *Greenland*, because of its green coasts. The sagas tell us he thought the fine name would tempt people to go there with him and see it for themselves.

The name Eric had chosen was a good description of the new country. The land around the Greenland fiords was indeed green. Driftwood, a most important commodity to settlers in northern lands, was in far better supply than in Iceland. Eric could truthfully report fishing and hunting as being excellent. There were also plenty

Left: Brattahlid (steep slope) was
the site of Eric the Red's farm. It was
in the part of Greenland later called
the Eastern Settlement. A second Norse
base was called the Western Settlement.
Above: this bear, carved from the
ivory tusk of a walrus, was found
at a farm on the Western Settlement.
It is apparently a child's toy.

of eider ducks, whose down was so highly valued by all Norsemen.

When, therefore, Eric led his party of would-be colonists to
Greenland in the summer of 986, those who reached it were not
disappointed by what they found. The sagas disagree about the
number of ships that set out on the venture from Iceland—one says
35 ships, another 25. But they agree that only 14 of them got safely to
Greenland. The ships were very heavily laden, and some probably
had to return to Iceland, unable to finish the journey. Others presumably were lost in the stormy, icy waters off the southern tip of
Greenland.

The number of pioneer settlers has been estimated at between 400
and 500. As Eric had been before and knew the country, he was able
to advise on the best places to settle. The majority pushed some 40
miles inland from the rocky coast and made their homes around the
heads of the fiords. The main center of habitation came to be known

as the Eastern Settlement—in the region of the modern port of Julianehåb. We know from the wealth of archaeological remains in the area and from the sagas that, at its height, the Eastern Settlement consisted of 190 farms, 12 churches, a cathedral, a monastery, and a convent. Because of his previous visit, Eric was recognized as head of the colony. He built himself a large house called Brattahlid at the head of the fiord he had named after himself. Modern visitors to the site of his farm at Brattahlid have remarked on the beauty of its setting and the richness of the land surrounding it.

Others among the first immigrants moved north up the coast to found the Western Settlement, around Godthåb Fiord. Summer after summer, encouraged by glowing reports from friends or relations who had gone ahead, more families arrived, and both settlements expanded and throve. A Norwegian, writing in the first half of the 1200's, gives the following account of Greenland in his time: "The people in that country are few, for only a small part is sufficiently free from ice to be habitable, but the people are all Christians and have churches and priests. If the land lay near to some other country it might be reckoned a third of a bishopric, but the Greenlanders now have their own bishop, as no other arrangement is possible on account of the great distance from other people. You ask what the inhabitants live on in that country since they sow no grain, but men can live on other food than bread. It is reported that the pasturage is

Above: ruins of the Norse cathedral built at Gardar, Eastern Settlement, in the 1100's. Today it is called Igaliko (great cooking place), the name given it by the Eskimos after the Vikings had departed.

Left: this amusing woodcut shows a fight between a Greenlander and an Eskimo. Eskimos arrived in Greenland more than a thousand years ago, and Eskimo attacks may have been responsible for the demise of the Norse settlements in that country.

good and that there are large and fine farms in Greenland. The farmers raise cattle and sheep in large numbers and make butter and cheese in great quantities. The people subsist chiefly on these foods and on beef, but they also eat the flesh of various kinds of game such as reindeer, whales, seals, and bears."

The Greenland colony survived for more than 400 years. In 1261, Greenland became the farthest outpost of the Norwegian empire. Norwegian ships made annual journeys between the two countries bringing the supplies of grain the Greenlanders needed. The colonists handed over walrus tusks, bearskins, and sealskins in exchange. Then, sometime in the early 1400's, the ships stopped coming and the Greenland colony died out. Perhaps it disappeared as a result of an epidemic, or fell to an Eskimo attack, or perhaps the end came about because of a worsening of the always harsh climate. There is no way of knowing.

Vikings reach North America

4

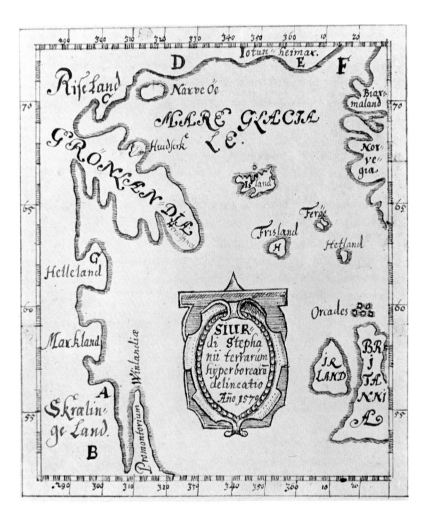

For more than 700 years, saga accounts of how Vikings reached North America, written down around 1200, were considered the products of imagination. However, with the general growth of scholarly and archaeological study and interest in the past, which took place in the 1800's and first half of the 1900's, there developed an increasingly large school of experts who believed strongly in the Viking achievements but who could produce no real evidence to support their theories. Then, in the early 1960's, a Norwegian archaeologist named Helge Ingstad discovered a site in northern Newfoundland that almost exactly fits a saga description of a

Above left: a Danish map of the North Atlantic, dated 1570, showing—more or less accurately—the British Isles, Shetlands, Orkneys, Faeroes, and Iceland. Greenland is linked to the American mainland, which includes Vinland, Markland, and Helluland, although they had long been deserted.

Above: dawn in Newfoundland. Relics of Viking settlements have been found here, indicating that the Norsemen reached America many centuries before Christopher Columbus 'discovered' it.

Viking settlement. Examination of the remains of buildings, tools, weapons, and other objects found on the site, verified Ingstad's contention that it dates from the 900's and 1000's, the period of Viking exploration westward. It now seems certain that the Vikings did indeed reach North America some 500 years before Columbus.

There are two versions of the story about discoveries of the land beyond Greenland, one in the *Greenlander's Saga*, and one in *Eric the Red's Saga*. One saga cannot be regarded as an any more reliable account than the other, but each must be looked upon as a sort of historical novel rather than an accurate record of facts.

According to the *Greenlander's Saga*, Bjarni Herjulfsson discovered the shores of North America quite by chance. Bjarni was a merchant shipowner who plied a regular route between Norway and Iceland. In the summer of 986, Bjarni set out from Norway with goods destined for his father in Iceland. Arriving there, he found that his father had gone with Eric the Red to Greenland. Bjarni and his men agreed to go in search of his father and they set off at once.

All went well for three days, until the wind dropped and a dense fog came down. The foul weather persisted for a further three days, and the sailors had no idea where they were. Then the fog lifted and the sun came out. Sails were hoisted and within a day the ship came in sight of land. Bjarni sailed in close to the coast and caught sight of low, forest-covered hills. Turning northward, he sailed on, and two days later reached another land. Bjarni had never seen Greenland, but he had heard about it, and he knew this could not possibly be it, since there were no glaciers. The boat drew closer to the shore and the voyagers saw that the land was flat and wooded. The wind dropped and the crew suggested going ashore for wood and water, but Bjarni forbade them, saying sharply, "You lack for neither." Once again they hoisted sail, and a southwest wind took them three days' distance before they saw land for the third time.

This time they saw a mountainous and glaciered land. Again, in spite of the entreaties of his crew, Bjarni refused to land. Consequently he lost his chance to become the first European to set foot on North American soil. Both Bjarni and his crew traveled back until they reached Herjulfsness in Greenland, where Bjarni's father lived. Here Bjarni settled down.

Some 14 years later, probably in the year 1000, Bjarni visited a jarl, called Eric, in Norway and told him of the three lands he had seen on his travels. Many who heard Bjarni's story were confounded by his lack of enterprise. Why had he not landed and explored the unknown countries? His words fired the imagination of many of the land-hungry Norsemen.

In Greenland, Leif, son of Eric the Red, heard Bjarni's account and determined to see the new lands for himself. He traveled to Herjulfsness, bought Bjarni's ship from him, and gathered together a willing crew of 35. Leif wanted his father to lead the expedition. Eric was reluctant, but agreed to go. On the way to the ship, however, Eric was injured in a fall from his horse and, considering the injury a bad omen, returned to his home, leaving Leif to lead the voyage.

Leif's expedition first reached land at the third of the countries Bjarni had sighted. They anchored the ship and rowed ashore in the ship's boat. The land was utterly barren, with glaciers in every direction. Leif named the area Helluland (flatstone land). Most authorities agree that this was the southern part of Baffin Island, though some believe it to have been Labrador or Newfoundland. Leif and his crew went back on board and sailed to the second land Bjarni had talked of. This was low and wooded, and white sandy beaches ran down to the sea. Leif called this region Markland (wood-

Above: blacksmith's tools, dating from the time of the Vikings' Atlantic voyages. The tools include pincers, a file, cutters, and a hammer head. The Greenland smithies turned out farming implements as well as weapons.

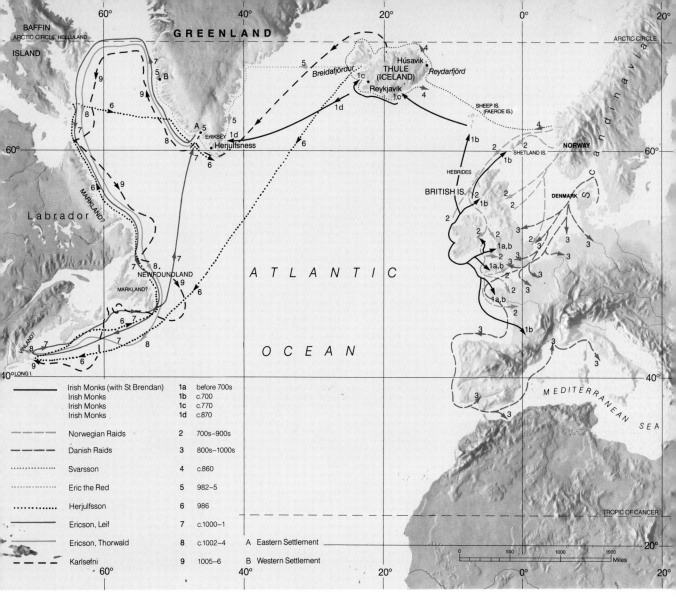

Irish Monks (with St Brendan)	1a	before 700s
Irish Monks	1b	c.700
Irish Monks	1c	c.770
Irish Monks	1d	c.870
Norwegian Raids	2	700s–900s
Danish Raids	3	800s–1000s
Svarsson	4	c.860
Eric the Red	5	982–5
Herjulfsson	6	986
Ericson, Leif	7	c.1000–1
Ericson, Thorwald	8	c.1002–4
Karlsefni	9	1005–6

A Eastern Settlement
B Western Settlement

Above: this map of the North Atlantic Ocean gives a clear idea of the enormous distances covered by the mariners of the Middle Ages, from the Irish monks in their flimsy keelless coracles to the Vikings in their long ships.
The green areas indicate the regions explored by the Irish and the Vikings during this period, though many of the actual landing places in North America are still uncertain.

Left: a painting from a church roof, dating from the 1300's, showing a boatload of Vikings. This double-ended vessel, with sail, is similar to that used by Bjarni Herjulfsson on the voyage when he accidentally discovered the coast of North America.

Above: a statue of the Viking Leif Ericson, in Iceland's capital of Reykjavik. Leif, son of Eric the Red, was probably the first European ever to set foot on American soil, shortly after the year 1000.

land)—it may have been Labrador, Newfoundland, or even Nova Scotia. Once again underway, Leif and his crew sailed with a north-east wind for two days before sighting land. They went ashore on an island which lay just north of a cape, and found lush grass. Returning to the ship, they sailed through the channel west around the cape and up a river. They moored in a lake and built temporary shelters. Later they built a more solid house and decided to winter there.

The salmon in the river were plentiful and larger than any the explorers had seen. The climate of the land was so mild that they had no need to prepare cattle fodder for the winter. During the winter, daylight lasted longer than in Iceland or Greenland. On the shortest day of winter, the sun was still visible in the middle of the afternoon as well as at breakfast time—a story detail which is one of the clues to mapping the settlement.

Once the house was built, Leif decided to divide his company into two groups, one to stay behind at the house while the other went out exploring the countryside. One evening when both groups were together in the house, they realized that one of their number, Tyrkir, a German, was missing. Leif was most upset because Tyrkir was his foster father. Before an organized search party had set out, however, Tyrkir returned, babbling with excitement.

Tyrkir had apparently found vines and grapes. Leif, however, was unwilling to believe him. Tyrkir assured him that he knew what he was talking about—he did, after all, come from a wine-making country. The mystery of what these "grapes" were has not been satisfactorily solved. Many explanations have been put forward. Some scholars say that "grapes" is a mistranslation for "grasses," others that global climate changes since Leif's time make it quite feasible that at one time grapes grew farther north than they now do. There are countless other suggestions, and no general agreement has been reached.

Leif set his men to cutting the vines, whatever they were, and to collecting the so-called grapes. These were stored in the ship's boat. Next spring the men made ready to sail, and they all returned to Greenland. Leif gave the new land the name of Vinland (wineland). It is now thought that Vinland was situated somewhere between Newfoundland to the north and Long Island to the south. Much discussion and argument has arisen as to exactly where it was, but, although many claims are made, there is no undeniable proof of Vinland's exact position.

In about 1002, Leif's brother Thorwald borrowed a ship and set out for Vinland. Leif was kept at home by affairs in the Greenland colony. Nothing of Thorwald's journey is recorded before the arrival at Leifsbudir—Leif's house—where the party encamped for the winter. In the spring, a group set out westward by boat and explored several islands. Except for a wooden grain store, they saw no signs of human habitation. This may have been built by the Algonkian Indians, who had such wooden granaries. Thorwald and his men

Above: clusters of wild grapes of the type known to have abounded on the Northeastern coast of America when Leif Ericson landed on the fertile land he named Vinland.

Right: Olaus Magnus' woodcut of 1555, shows the Vikings catching salmon. The fish caught by Leif and his comrades in Vinland were, according to the sagas, the largest they had ever seen.

returned to Leifsbudir in the autumn.

The following summer, Thorwald set off eastward and then north along the coast. His ship was caught in a gale which broke the keel and drove it onto a cape. Calling the spot Kjalarnes (keel cape), the sailors remained there to repair the ship.

From the cape, they then sailed due east into the mouth of a fiord, a place Thorwald thought very beautiful—so beautiful that he told his men he would like to make his home there. On a stretch of sand inside the headland the travelers came across three boats made from

Above: Olaus Magnus' book contains many scenes of everyday life, like this one of Vikings repairing a boat.

Above right: an assortment of Viking weapons (swords and a spearhead), and a stirrup, all showing the solid quality of their ironwork.

animal skins. Underneath each boat were three sleeping men. The men from the sea killed all but one of the sleepers, whom they described as *Skraelings*, a word used in the sagas to describe the natives of different countries. These may have been Algonkian Indians—Jacques Cartier, a later French explorer, noted the habit of American Indians to sleep under overturned boats when traveling.

Thorwald's party walked up onto the headland and saw many mounds which they took to be human habitations. Then, the saga says, overtaken by a great drowsiness, the Norsemen fell asleep. All at once they were wakened by a loud noise and looking about them saw Skraeling canoes putting out from the opposite shore. The Skraelings fired arrows at the Norsemen and then withdrew. But one of their arrows mortally wounded Thorwald. As he died, he entreated his men to bury him at the headland he had selected for his home, and to call the place thenceforth Krossanes—cross cape.

An arrowhead of the type used by the Indians was found in the 1930's by a Danish archaeologist in a churchyard in Greenland. Some experts think it the very weapon which slew Thorwald, perhaps carried back by his shocked followers.

When Thorwald's brother Thorstein heard about Thorwald's death, he decided to go to Vinland to fetch the body. But this expedition was storm-tossed all summer and never left Greenland waters. During a winter spent at the Western Settlement, many, including Thorstein, died of sickness. Thorstein's widow Gudrid took his body back to Eriksfjord for burial.

In the summer of 1005, a ship from Iceland brought Thorfinn Karlsefni, an Icelandic merchant, to Greenland. He stayed with Leif at Brattahlid and married the widow Gudrid that winter. Gudrid urged Karlsefni to go to Vinland, and when he agreed they sailed off with 160 men, 5 women, and some livestock. When they arrived safely at Leifsbudir they found a stranded whale, which kept them well supplied with food. Fishing and hunting generally were good.

Left: this Indian arrowhead made of Labrador quartzite was found in a churchyard in Greenland, and is claimed to be from the very arrow that killed Leif Ericson's brother Thorwald in Vinland.

Below: a statue of Thorfinn Karlsefni, who tried to establish a permanent colony in North America. The statue stands in Fairmount Park, Philadelphia.

Next summer, the settlers made contact with the Skraelings, who were much frightened by a bull the Norsemen had brought with them. The Skraelings gave the Norsemen furs in exchange for food, and then went away.

Karlsefni built a stockade around his house in preparation for the Skraelings' next visit. Before it was completed, his wife Gudrid gave birth to a son, Snorri, who can lay claim to being the first European born on American soil. On their next visit to the encampment, the Skraelings tried to steal the Greenlanders' weapons and a skirmish ensued. The third encounter between Indians and settlers led to more serious fighting. This time Karlsefni, deciding that the new country's disadvantages outweighed its advantages, ordered his men to load up the ship, and the party returned to Greenland.

The next initiator of a Vinland voyage was a woman. Freydis, a daughter of Eric the Red, persuaded two brothers from Norway to

Above: this toy Viking ship, seen alongside a real one, was found in the ruins of a bathhouse in Greenland's Western Settlement.

Right: some fine examples of Viking jewelry—two gold brooches, a twisted gold wire ring, and (at top) a silver ring and necklace, with a pendant in the shape of Thor's hammer.

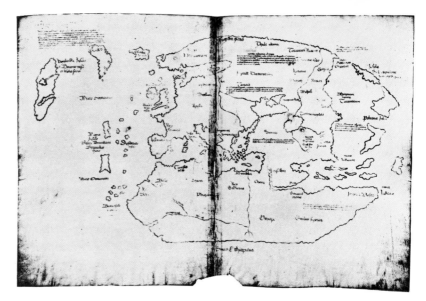

Right: the celebrated Vinland map, found in Geneva in 1957 and now at Yale University, gave further evidence of Viking explorations in North America. It shows the Old World —with Europe's size greatly exaggerated at Asia's expense—and the outlines of three islands, Iceland, Greenland, and Vinland. The inscription tells how Bjarni Herjulfsson and Leif Ericson discovered Vinland, and how Leif named it for the vines there.

sail to Leifsbudir with her and her husband. Each party took with them 30 men and their womenfolk. They arrived at Leifsbudir, where Freydis moved into Leif's old house and the brothers built another. A quarrel broke out between the two houses, and Freydis goaded her husband into killing the two brothers and their men. Then Freydis took an ax and dealt with the women herself. Early in the spring she and her husband loaded the ships and sailed back to Greenland.

According to *Eric the Red's Saga*, it was Leif Ericson, not Bjarni Herjulfsson, who first discovered Vinland. *Eric the Red's Saga* was probably written down later than the *Greenlander's Saga*. It is more fanciful, and most scholars take it as a variation on the theme, arising out of the many stories that circulated about the Vinland voyages between 980 and 1020.

One episode of *Eric the Red's Saga* describes Thorfinn Karlsefni's voyage. In this version his party followed the by now traditional route to Leifsbudir, and on the way found the keel of a ship at a place they called Keel Cape. To the south they could see the Atlantic shoreline's seemingly endless beaches, which they named Furdustrandir—wonder beaches.

The party continued to sail parallel with the beaches until they discovered a bay. There they put ashore a Scottish couple, named Hake and Hekja, to explore the land. In three days the couple came back bringing with them ears of wild wheat. The whole expedition set off again and sailed into a fiord indented with bays and streams which they named Straumfjord. Landing to explore the terrain, Karlsefni's men found it mountainous and very beautiful.

The winter which followed their landfall was harsh. The Norsemen had done nothing to prepare for it. Hunting and fishing were impossible. Ten of the would-be colonists resolved to turn back. But their voyage ended badly. They were caught in a storm and driven across the Atlantic to Ireland. There they were captured by the inhabitants of the land and forced into slavery. Thorhall, the

Above: a painting by an unknown artist of the 1600's of two American Indians. The Indians, who were called *Skraelings* (foreigners) by the Vikings, attacked the Norse settlements. After the Vikings left, no white man set foot on Indian territory until the 1400's.

leader of the group, died while he was still a slave of the Irish.

The rest of the colonists went on south with Karlsefni. They established a base at a place they called Hop (landlocked bay). Early one morning, nine skin canoes arrived. Their crews carried staves which they whirled in the air with a threshing noise. The canoeists landed, surveyed the Norsemen with astonishment, stayed a while, and then paddled away.

The Norsemen spent the winter at Hop, where the weather was very mild. One spring morning, another fleet of canoes arrived and the strangers came ashore and bartered skins and fur for red cloth, which they seemed to prize. A bull belonging to one of Karlsefni's men bellowed at them so loudly that the terrified Skraelings left in a great hurry. Some days later, a vast horde of Skraeling canoes arrived and there was a fierce battle. In *Eric the Red's Saga*, Freydis saved the day by slapping her sword on her breast which frightened the Skraelings away.

In ever-diminishing prosperity and numbers, the Greenland settlements hung on, the Western Settlement for 350 years, the

Above: this painting of a Mandan village shows coracle-like boats in the foreground. Legend has it that the Mandan, a Sioux tribe of American Indians, were visited by Welshmen, who were familiar with such boats. There is no historical proof of this, but the similarity between the word for coracle in Welsh and Mandan suggests there may be truth in the story.

Eastern a little longer. During that time it is very likely that traders and other sailors were blown off course to America just as Bjarni Herjulfsson had been. The Greenlanders themselves must often have crossed to Markland in search of much needed timber, as they used up their own supplies of driftwood. One source relates that a ship from Greenland was blown by a storm to Iceland after having visited Markland in 1347.

Archaeologists have unearthed various objects suggesting that Scandinavian settlement in North America may have penetrated some way inland. A theory enthusiastically supported by a small number of scholars—that a young Welsh prince named Madoc reached American shores in 1170—must remain only a story, as there is no conclusive proof.

At present, all that can be said is that, with the exception of the voyage to Markland in 1347, Freydis' expedition was the last journey of discovery and exploration by the Norsemen in North America. Nearly 150 years were to pass before Christopher Columbus' voyage again aroused European interest in the New World.

Right: the Mongolian steppes. These vast expanses of grassland are inhabited by nomads who move constantly from place to place, with their horses, sheep, and cattle, in search of fresh pastures.

Below: a modern Mongol, descendant of the fierce warriors of Genghis Khan. Like his ancestors, he rides a pony.

Genghis Khan and the Mongols

5

The Irish and Viking voyages in the North Atlantic Ocean made the peoples of Europe aware for the first time that the world did not end at Europe's western shores. They now knew that there were lands farther to the west that could be reached in a few days' sailing, and which had all the necessities to support life. But, even in the 1200's, the Eastern lands remained a mystery to Europeans. However, events were taking place in the East that forced the Europeans to look outward, and effectively ended their isolation from the rest of the world for ever.

The nomadic tribes of central Asia, the Tartars, Merkids, Kereyids, Mongols, and others, were made up of hardy people who had to struggle for survival against a harsh climate and warlike neighbors. When drought struck their sparse, ill-watered grasslands north of the great Gobi Desert, or when winters were severe, the nomads had to raid their more civilized neighbors in order to survive. Sometimes the raiders would settle and be absorbed in the civilization they attacked. More often they withdrew to the grassy plains of their homeland—until the next famine came.

The only major civilization within easy reach was that of China. The Chinese, protected from attack by the Great Wall they had built in the northern part of their empire to stop marauding tribes, were usually safe. The Mongol tribes were weakened and divided by constant skirmishes and blood feuds. Long-time masters of political manipulation, the Chinese had also worked out a successful technique for keeping the Mongols at bay. "Set a barbarian to control a barbarian," was their motto. They would make alliances with some tribes, supporting them in their wars and blood feuds, in return for service in defense of the Chinese Empire.

Sometimes the Chinese were very weak and the tribes grew powerful enough to turn and sweep down on the empire itself, ousting and supplanting the ruling dynasty. This happened in the early 900's A.D., when the Khitan tribes took northern China and established the Liao (iron) dynasty. Khitan is the origin of the word *Cathay*, the ancient name for China. Between A.D. 1114 and 1125, the Juchen ousted the Liao from northern China and established the Chin dynasty there. From this comes the name *China*.

That might have been the pattern for centuries to come but for the birth, c. 1162, of one of the most remarkable men in history—a man whose conquests were to make so deep a mark on the story of Asia

and Russia that the worst scars are only now being effaced. That man was Genghis Khan.

In 1167, Yesugai Baghutur, chief of the obscure Kiyad tribe of northeastern Mongolia, was returning from a battle against his neighbors, a Tartar tribe. Thirty years earlier, the Tartars had betrayed to the Chinese the chief of a tribe allied by blood to the Kiyads. Now, by way of revenge, Yesugai had taken a Tartar chief, Temujin. On his return home, Yesugai found that his wife had borne him a son. According to custom, he called the boy Temujin, to give him the valor and courage of the captured chief. This was the boy who was to grow up to become Genghis Khan.

Every young chieftain intended to be successful, or at least valiant, in war, and so to sustain the honor of his tribe. But from very early days, Temujin was determined to do much more. He never deviated from his aim to unite all the Mongol tribes, to weld them into a massive, loyal, invincible army, and then to force easy and regular tribute from every surrounding civilization—China, the Khorezm Empire (western Turkistan and parts of Iran) and Russia.

To medieval Westerners, Genghis Khan was an ignorant, brutal savage. Popular opinion has only slightly mellowed with time, and it was not until modern times that scholars began to reveal the full extent of his political and military genius.

From the start, Temujin realized that he would have to break up the existing petty clan loyalties and feuds of his countrymen and replace them with a greater all-Mongol loyalty. He saw that the best way to do this was not by the use of military might alone, but also by exercising political tact. He would use existing customs that helped his aims and he would devalue and destroy customs that ran counter to them. Warfare, much as he loved a good battle, was little use without political craftsmanship.

There were two tribal institutions that Temujin seized upon and encouraged in every possible way. The first was the Mongol custom of one warrior (*nukur*) freely binding himself to the service of another. The binding oath took precedence over all other claims of loyalty, even those of tribe and marriage. The other institution was that of the protected or subordinate tribe—a system whereby a tribe voluntarily put itself under the protection of a powerful neighbor, performing vassal-like services in return for that protection. Often the superior tribe took advantage of the arrangement and oppressed

Above: a portrait of Genghis Khan in later life, from a Chinese album of emperors, dating from the 1200's.

its vassals. It was then no dishonor if the protected tribe deserted its guardians, even at the height of battle. Temujin owed several early victories to such desertions in his favor.

Though Temujin had as yet no way of knowing it, these institutions were very similar to those of chivalry and feudalism in Europe at that time. Because of the similarity, the earliest travelers from Europe felt surprisingly at home among the Mongols, despite the many strange, wonderful, and terrible things they saw and heard.

In fostering these institutions, Temujin inevitably weakened the

Above: this Mongol painting, dating from the 1400's, shows scenes in a nomad camp. Both men and animals are skillfully, if not realistically, drawn.

older tribal and blood brother loyalties of the nomads. He also destroyed the system whereby all the more powerful tribes had "left-hand" and "right-hand" branches, and power passed, by custom, from one branch to the other at each generation.

In three decades of such political maneuvering, using what institutions he could, along with an unhesitating, ruthless use of military might, Temujin turned the divided and scattered Mongol tribes into some of the most efficient, loyal, and fearsome warriors the world has ever known. He was no mere opportunist. The rigid code of loyalty he was trying to instil into his people always came first, and no one stuck to it more strictly than he.

Again and again contemporary records tell how Temujin praised men who deserted to him but refused to betray their former masters. If a deserter did betray his master, Temujin accepted the betrayal but always executed the betrayer. At a more political level, he never turned against an ally merely because the time to do so was ripe and the chance at hand. He would maneuver and scheme until

he could accuse the unwanted ally, man, or tribe, of disloyalty. That way he could justify his action in terms of the common good, perhaps win over some of his opponent's supporters—and above all teach everyone a lesson in building up the new all-Mongol spirit and forgetting old quarrels.

In 1206, Temujin, already a *khan* (chief) of the Mongols, was formally proclaimed *Genghis* Khan. The word comes from Turkic *tingiz*, meaning *ocean*. The Mongols thought the world was flat and surrounded by water—hence Genghis Khan meant universal ruler or king of kings. It was at this time that Genghis Khan began in earnest his career of world conquest.

Genghis Khan soon showed how brilliantly he could create new military forms to fit his new needs. He ensured a more loyal and efficient army around 1203 by creating an elite bodyguard, which, while a unit of the regular army, was under his personal command. Many of the guards were sons of generals and military governors and as such were hostages for their parents' good behavior. Like any

Above: in this picture, a Mongol warrior plaits the tail of his horse. His Chinese-patterned cloak is held in place by an ornate belt, and his golden helmet is lined with costly fur.

feudal chief, Genghis Khan rewarded service and victory with grants of land and people. The people thus given to a warlord soon learned that their loyalty belonged to him, not to earlier allies and kinsfolk, who now might "belong" to another lord.

In little over 30 years, Genghis Khan had created one efficient political unit. Such a system had taken European countries centuries to achieve. Moreover, he had done it without benefit of writing or of a single, organizing religion. Nevertheless, even this achievement was nothing compared with what was to follow during his *khanate*.

Europe, as yet, knew nothing of the changes that were taking place in the East. But among the merchants of the Moslem world—Persians, Turks, and Arabs—the knowledge was widespread. Moslem merchants traveled in Asia—to northern China, then ruled by the Chin dynasty, and southern China, under the rule of the Sung dynasty; to Hsi Hsia; India; Khorezm; and southern Russia. From them Genghis Khan learned of the wealthy civilizations to the west. He also knew of the literate Uigur and other Turkic nomads living in the areas between his lands and the source of the great wealth. He saw that to exploit the westward possibilities for booty and tribute, he would have to make use of these nomads. Traveling merchants played a vital part in the expansion of Genghis Khan's empire, first as his spies, then as informal and formal ambassadors, and finally as administrators and governors of the enlarged empire.

Genghis Khan developed his military technology, too. The traditional nomad army had a limited, though terrifying, arsenal. Tactics centered on the cavalry and their tough little ponies. Each rider had four to six ponies, any one of which could carry him up to 100 miles in a day. By rotating his choice of mount, the rider could ensure that each animal carried only light equipment, food, and tents for three

Above left: this large stone tortoise once supported a column, on which was probably inscribed helpful information for travelers. Such aids were of great use to travelers journeying through the vast Mongol Empire.

to five days between each man-carrying ride. In this way, the cavalry could cover huge distances at unprecedented speeds, and strike, conquer, and loot, before either pressing on or vanishing back into the apparently endless steppes (the vast plains of Asia). The foot soldiers of the khan's armies, too, were used to long marches and quick strikes.

For those small, self-reliant units, a favorite tactic was to feign retreat and draw the enemy after them, then to wheel about, re-form, and annihilate the astonished pursuers. These were adequate tactics for hit-and-run border raiders, but they were hardly world-beating. Genghis Khan, realizing this, recruited the best Hsia and Chinese military engineers, and, as his empire grew, called upon Persian and Khorezmian engineers as well. Within the space of just over 10 years, he had transformed Mongol military tactics as thoroughly as he had the structure of their society.

Above: Genghis Khan (with scepter) pictured outside his tent. Like all feudal lords, he gave his subjects gifts of land and property, but in return he demanded willing service and absolute loyalty to the empire.

Armies in the field fell before Genghis Khan's cavalry and foot soldiers. Fortified towns were no more secure. His forces battered them with catapults and other devices, tunneled under their walls, and blew them down with gunpowder.

With these armies and tactics, Genghis Khan mastered most of central Asia by about 1225. As early in his career as 1215, Genghis' forces had captured Cambaluc (modern Peking), and extended their rule over most of northern China and Manchuria. After taking Cambaluc, Genghis Khan turned his attention to the west, and between 1215 and 1222, subdued first eastern Turkestan and then the Khorezm Empire, the greatest Moslem power in central Asia. Then he sent one band of troops to pursue the defeated Khorezmians across the Hindu Kush down into northwest India, and another band around the south of the Caspian Sea through Georgia and the Caucasus into southern Russia.

Genghis Khan died in 1227, several years after his forces, or hordes as they came to be called, had laid waste and terrorized much of southern Russia and the Volga Valley. Hardly a whisper of their activities filtered through to western Europe, though. Perhaps that is why the effects of these terrible atrocities have at times been underestimated in Europe.

Southern Russia at that time was as economically advanced as the other countries of eastern Europe. It had well-developed towns with skilled workers and a growing middle class of merchants and tradesmen. During the period of occupation the Mongols destroyed it all. They replaced it with their own system of absolute rule, by which tax-gathering princes lived off crushed and obedient peasants. It was more than 200 years before Russia became even as prosperous as it

Above: Genghis Khan's cavalry had no equal in its time, and his men delighted in showing off their individual skills, circus-fashion, as depicted in this copy of a Chinese painting.

Right: modern Mongolians are still proud of their horsemanship. Here contestants assemble for the start of a horse race. Their mounts, similar to those that carried the Mongols across Asia and into Europe over 700 years ago, are stocky and tough.

Above: the death of Genghis Khan. Mourners gather around the bier of their great chief, who died during a campaign against the neighboring kingdom of Tanggut. His death was hastened by the effect of a fall from horseback while out hunting.

had been in 1220, by which time western Europe had moved well ahead.

Until after the death of Genghis Khan, western Europe heard nothing of the Mongols and their empire, save news of a great Mongol victory over the Russians on the banks of the Dnepr in 1240. The empire had by then stabilized lands south and east of the Caspian Sea and the Urals. When Genghis Khan died, one of his four sons, Ogotai, continued the expansion of Mongol rule farther into China, the Middle East, and through Russia into the countries of eastern Europe.

Europe could hardly fail now to hear about the ferocious Mongols —the Tartars, as the Europeans called them. In 1238, Ogotai's armies crossed Russia and by 1241 they had penetrated as far as what is now Poland, Czechoslovakia, and Hungary. Nothing could stop them. Even the heavily armed Teutonic Knights, much feared by infidels (unbelievers) in the Crusades, were ignominiously defeated by Mongol troops at the Battle of Liegnitz in 1241.

The Mongols' reputation raced on before them. As early as 1238, while the hordes had still only reached southern Russia, the English chronicler Matthew Paris recorded that fear of the Mongols prevented the people of Gotland (in the Baltic Sea off southern Sweden), and Friesland (part of The Netherlands) from coming to England for the herring catch. As a result, herrings were so plentiful that year that they could be bought very cheaply, even far inland. Even today the memory of the Mongol hordes lingers on in eastern Europe, where "Tartars" are still the bogeymen of many favorite children's stories. The years between 1238 and 1241 must have been terrible times to print themselves so indelibly on people's memories.

In the West, one or two of the more astute rulers got the first glimmerings of the dangers that hung over them. A mission from Syria, which had suffered Mongol attacks, came to the English and French courts with proposals for a Moslem-Christian alliance against the Mongols. Nothing came of the request, but it helped to spread accounts of the awful devastation the Mongols left in their wake. The other nations of western Europe were divided by a quarrel between the pope of the time and the Holy Roman Emperor Frederick II, and they were also involved in plans for Crusades. In the event, western Europe was saved from a concentrated Mongol onslaught, which it was probably in no condition to resist, by the fortuitous death of Ogotai and the quarrels this caused among the other Mongol chieftains. After Ogotai's death in 1241, most of the Mongol leaders, including the generals in charge of the European campaign, hurried back to Karakoram, their capital in Mongolia. They were anxious to take part in the election of the next Great Khan—a process that could take years.

Giving up their campaign in Europe meant little to the generals. They had met no serious opposition and felt they could resume and swiftly conclude their conquest of Europe at any time. Europe, knowing nothing of the death of Ogotai, or its significance, could not understand why the Mongols had suddenly withdrawn. But they made no use of the respite they had so unexpectedly been granted. Instead, they continued to devote their attention to their internal affairs and to the papal-imperial quarrel, until a new pope, Innocent IV, was elected in 1243. This pope did two things about the Mongol problem. At a meeting of the papal general council he supported a decision to advise Christians to "block every road or passage" by which the enemy could pass ". . . by means of ditches, walls, build-

Above: Souboutai, the war general of Genghis Khan, seen here in fighting regalia. Souboutai led the Great Khan's armies into southern Russia, paving the way for Batu, Genghis Khan's grandson, to set up the Golden Horde there around 1240.

Above: Western fears of the 'yellow peril' from the Orient date from the years of the Mongol conquests. Cruel though they could be, the Mongols' bloodthirsty tendencies were often exaggerated, as in Matthew Paris' *Chronica Maiora,* where they are depicted as brutal torturers and killers.

Left: a realistic picture of two nomad travelers in conversation. It was only after the Mongol invasion of Russia that Europeans saw for themselves what the Mongols were really like, and discovered the rich, advanced civilization of the Eastern lands.

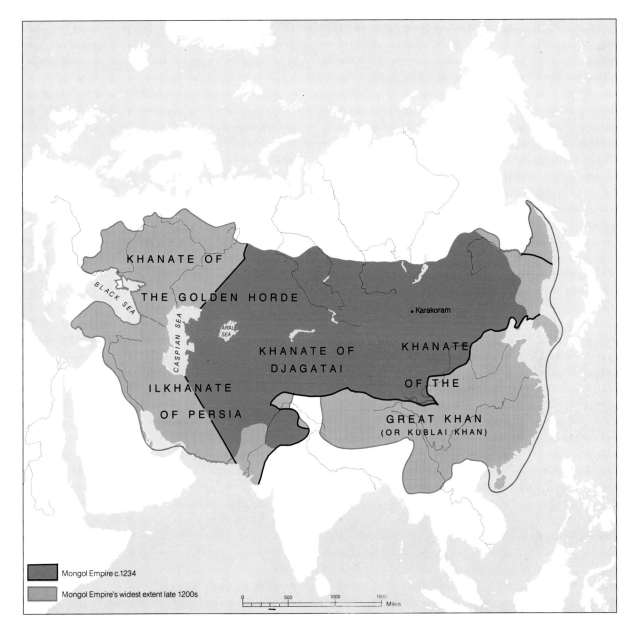

KHANATE OF

THE GOLDEN HORDE

BLACK SEA

CASPIAN SEA

ARAL SEA

KHANATE OF
DJAGATAI

• Karakoram

KHANATE

ILKHANATE

OF THE

OF PERSIA

GREAT KHAN
(OR KUBLAI KHAN)

Mongol Empire c.1234

Mongol Empire's widest extent late 1200s

0   500   1000   1500
                    Miles

ings, or other contrivances," and agreed that the church would help to foot the bills. More significantly, Innocent sent two parties of missionaries to the Mongol chiefs with letters exhorting them to "give over their bloody slaughter of mankind and to receive the Christian faith." As well as delivering the letters, the missionaries were to find out as much as possible about the strength and character of the Mongol Empire and bring the information back to the West.

One party, led by Friar Lawrence of Portugal, has left no record of its journey. Of the other, under Giovanni de Piano Carpini, we have his own firsthand account. His party not only reached the Mongol capital, Karakoram, a journey of some 6,000 miles overland, but had the good fortune to arrive during the final ceremonies for choosing the new Great Khan.

Above: this map of Asia shows the Mongol Empire in about 1234—a few years before Giovanni de Piano Carpini set out on his amazing journey to Karakoram. The map also shows the empire at its greatest extent in the late 1200's, when the Polos visited Kublai Khan at the new Mongol capital of Cambaluc. By this time, the Mongol possessions had been divided into four major khanates. Kublai Khan himself personally ruled in the eastern khanate of the Great Khan.

Envoys to the Great Khan

Friar Carpini seems to have been a most unlikely explorer. To begin with, he was more than 60 years old when he left Lyon at the start of his daunting journey. He was also an exceedingly fat man, and would have found the discomforts of the journey particularly severe. And Carpini had no knowledge at all of Asian languages. In Breslau he acquired an interpreter, Benedict of Poland, but Benedict turned out to be a very poor linguist. Communication with the strangers they met on the way was very difficult.

Carpini must have had buoyant courage and faith to be able to set off barefoot into the heart of the unknown barbarian world. Starting out with little more than the clothes they wore, he and his party traveled through many countries the Mongols had laid waste between Europe and Mongolia itself. They spent 16 months among fierce nomads, and survived periods of great deprivation and hardship. They brought back a most detailed account of Mongol society, law, costume, habits, diet, and, most important, military tactics and discipline. They also produced an accurate family tree of leading Mongols from Genghis Khan onward, and a list of all the important foreign ambassadors who brought presents to the new khan.

The letter Carpini was to take to the Great Khan was signed by the pope on March 9, 1245. On April 16, Easter Day, Carpini's party set off from Lyon in France where the pope was then living. As begging friars—they were Franciscans—Carpini, and his five

Left: Mongol warriors besieging a city. The Mongol Empire, under the successors of Genghis Khan, stretched from China westward into Asia Minor and the eastern countries of Europe.

Right: Friar Carpini, the Franciscan monk, who, as an elderly man, traveled from France across Asia to the court of Kuyuk Khan and back. The epic journey took him more than two years, and made him the first European to cross Asia.

Above: Pope Innocent IV, in 1245, summoned a general council of the church to debate measures to be taken against the continuing Mongol threat. Carpini's journey was made with the pope's blessing, to learn more of Mongol plans, and in the hope of converting the Mongols to Christianity. *(Bodleian Library, Oxford. MS. Canon. Pat. Lat. 144, fol. 1.)*

servants traveled mainly on the charity of people they encountered. Fortunately for them, to begin with they mainly encountered rich men—the kings, dukes, and bishops of Silesia, Bohemia, and other eastern European countries—who gave alms in generous quantities. The friars were, after all, the ambassadors of the pope himself.

At the start, for the 1200's, their journey was comfortable enough, and they learned a great deal about the Mongols from people they visited on the way. Everyone they met stressed that the envoys would get nowhere with the Mongols unless they were prepared to make ample use of gifts and bribes, so Carpini and his companions spent some of the alms they received on buying furs. These would be gifts luxurious enough to please the Mongols, but light enough to carry easily on horseback.

At the beginning of February, 1246, Carpini and the others reached the Dnepr River and the city of Kiev, which had been the chief city of Russia until a few years earlier. Now, "traveling through that country we found an innumerable multitude of dead men's skulls and bones lying upon the earth. For it was a very large and populous city, but it is now in a manner brought to nothing: For there do scarce remain 200 houses, the inhabitants whereof are kept in extreme bondage." Kiev and the district around the city had become part of the Mongol Empire in 1240, and had very soon dis-

Right: a farmhouse in Perugia, Italy. Carpini was born in 1182, in a village near Perugia, but spent most of his life teaching in northern Europe.

78

covered the harsh penalties involved in being ruled by the Mongols.

Carpini learned at this point that the large European horses his party had brought were quite unsuited to the journey across the steppes and deserts of Asia. From Kiev they would have to use the hardier Mongol ponies. Then Carpini and his followers set out into the vast Mongol-occupied Asian steppes, not knowing whether they were going to life or death. Soon they had their first encounter with the Mongols—Tartars, as the Europeans called them: ". . . armed Tartars came rushing upon us in uncivil and horrible manner . . . when we had [told] them that we were the pope's legates, receiving some victuals at our hands they immediately departed."

Although, according to Carpini, they were generally "uncivil," the Mongols of these first outposts gave the party Christian guides to escort them through the realms of a succession of lesser warlords to the court of Batu, a grandson of Genghis Khan. Batu was one of the

Above: an illustration from a book of journeys to the Orient, dating from the 1600's. This section deals with Carpini's mission and shows Mongols with their horses, fording a river.

Left: Batu, grandson of Genghis Khan, conquered almost the whole of Russia and formed the Golden Horde, the name given to the part of the Mongol Empire in Russia and Kazakhstan.

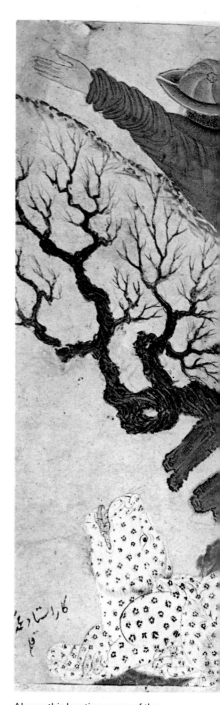

Above: this hunting scene of the 1400's shows four Mongol noblemen, with dogs and hawks, riding along the crest of a hill, while two leopards hide from them in the foreground.

greatest Mongol chiefs, and founder of the Golden Horde, which comprised southern Russia and Kazakhstan. Batu's encampment was on the lower Volga River. In Russia, Carpini and his party traveled through the Golden Horde, passing four mighty rivers on the way. Carpini was one of the first Europeans to identify these rivers by their Russian names as the Dnepr, the Don, the Volga, and the Iaec (Ural). He was wrong, however, in thinking that they all ran into the Black Sea. Having journeyed down the Dnepr (which was frozen over) for several days, the Christian party made for the Volga where they found Batu's encampment. He received them with reasonable graciousness, but forced them to take part in a ceremony which they must have found somewhat humiliating—purification by fire. No pain or danger was involved because they had only to pass between two widely spaced fires, but to medieval Christians fire was a purge for heretics and witches. It was, therefore, a strange ritual for the pope's own emissaries to be forced to perform.

With the help of Batu's most learned men, Carpini and Benedict translated the contents of the pope's letter into the Russian, Tartarian, and Saracen languages. Batu, Carpini says, "attentively noted" the contents. Although they had traveled long and hard to reach his camp, Batu then decided that the missionaries must go on almost at once to the court of Kuyuk, another grandson of Genghis and son of Ogotai, who was about to be elected the next Great Khan. Batu detained some of Carpini's servants, saying that he would

send them straight back to the pope with letters from Carpini telling of the good treatment Batu had given his party. In fact, as Carpini found on his return journey, the servants were kept inside Mongol borders.

On Easter Day, 1246, having said their prayers and taken a "slender" breakfast, Carpini's party set out on the most trying stage of their long journey. Carpini carefully noted the name of each lord or governor through whose territory they rode, but gives little description of the landscape. Perhaps there was not much to describe:

Above: a sensitive and highly stylized Chinese painting of two Mongols grooming their horses. The delicate treatment is typical of Chinese art throughout the centuries.

"Conditions were very wretched, and [we] found many skulls and bones of dead men lying upon the earth like a dunghill . . . we found innumerable cities with castles and many towns left desolate."

Crossing central Asia north of the Caspian Sea and the Aral Sea, with its long stretches of arid, desolate wasteland, Carpini's party reached the waters of the Syr Darya River. After following the course of the river for several hundred miles, the monotony of the flat, dry plain was broken by the cool peaks of the Tien Shan range. Their speed was impressive—all through this part of the journey Carpini and his men had to withstand the exhaustion of five or six changes of mount in a day.

The Mongol post-horse system was obviously already well

established at the time of Carpini's journey, although it had not yet reached its peak of efficiency. Toward the end of the 1200's, there were 10,000 way stations, some with only a few ponies, some with up to 400, all kept in constant readiness for couriers, ambassadors, and imperial officials. Using this system, riders could get from one end of the empire to the other in a couple of months. On major routes there would be way stations every three miles. Relays of couriers galloping from station to station could cover as much as 500 miles in 24 hours. The system was an ingenious extension of the nomad warrior's old system of traveling with a string of horses, and changing frequently from one to another.

Riding as rapidly as their ponies could trot, Carpini's mission

Above: a nomad taking his horse to graze. The different viewing angles convey a sense of movement—a contrast to the Chinese handling of a similar subject seen opposite.

traveled all day and often most of the night, "without eating anything and often we came so late to our lodgings that we had not
time to eat that night." During Lent and other periods of fasting,
the whole of their diet had been "nothing but millet with water and
salt . . . and we had nothing except snow melted in a kettle to drink."
Even when they were not observing religious fasts, Carpini's party
ate only enough to keep them alive. To travel so far on so little food
was a remarkable feat of endurance.

From the Tien Shan mountains, the mission journeyed to the
northeast toward the heights of the Tarbagati and Altai Mountains
where at the end of June, they experienced severe cold and a heavy
snowfall. They rode on, still at top speed, for about three weeks, and
"on the day of Mary Magdalene [July 22], arrived at the court of the
Emperor Elect [Kuyuk]." They had not actually reached Karakoram
but were at the summer court of Syra Orda, half a day's ride from the
capital. Kuyuk did not let them see Karakoram, which, as later
European visitors were to find, was a most unimpressive place.

The emperor elect kept the pope's envoys waiting a long time and
allowed them only a near-starvation diet. In the context of the
huge empire of which Kuyuk had just gained control, the Christians

Above: travelers at a wayside inn.
This Chinese painting is full of action and indicates that, although on
many occasions the early travelers
had to sleep in the open, they sometimes found lodgings for the night.

Right: an illustration of Carpini's
journey, showing the tent of the khan,
surrounded by a wooden stockade.

84

and their pope were very small fry and he saw no need to give the envoys a lavish welcome. He did, however, eventually allow the travelers the rare privilege of entering his tent—anyone who stepped into it uninvited was immediately beaten or put to death.

Carpini spent some of the time in the four months his company stayed at Syra Orda listening to court gossip. He succeeded in working out the relationships and intermarriages of all the descendants of Genghis Khan. The family tree he brought back to the West was so accurate that it has been improved on only during the past 150 years, and then only in minor details. Carpini learned, too, how busy Kuyuk was destroying all the subjects of his empire who had grown too powerful during Ogotai's more lenient rule. While he was at Kuyuk's court, the coronation of the khan took place. In his reports of the journey, Carpini describes the ceremony, which, with its splendid Oriental trappings, must have seemed strange and wonderful to the European travelers.

Just before Carpini and his two companions were to leave the court, Kuyuk Khan decided that he wanted to send Mongol ambassadors back with the Christians to the pope. Carpini was particularly anxious to avoid this. He did not want the khan's personal envoys to realize how weakened Europe was by internal strife, or to spy out Europe's limited resources. Carpini also realized that if the Mongol messengers should happen to be killed by Christians, the consequences for Europe could be appalling. Fortunately the question was dropped, and, in November, Carpini and his companions set out for home alone.

This journey was no less hard than the outward one. They traveled all winter long and the weather made the going very slow. At night the elderly friar and his companions lay "in the deserts oftentimes upon the snow, except with our feet we made a piece of ground bare to lie upon. For there were no trees but the plain champion [hedgeless] field. And oftentimes in the morning we found ourselves all covered with snow driven over us by the wind."

It was May 9, 1247, before they arrived back at Batu's camp on the Volga. From there they were given safe conduct to the Mongol borders, collecting their servants and year-old letters to Pope Innocent on the way. When they reached Kiev on June 9, the citizens rushed out to meet them with great joy "as over men who had been risen from death to life."

Carpini and Benedict reached the pope's court at Lyon in the autumn of 1247, and presented Kuyuk Khan's letter. This letter has been preserved in the Vatican vaults. The travelers told the story of their amazing pioneer journey, but their report contained little to relieve Europeans of their fears of the Mongols. Carpini's detailed and accurate review of Mongol life, politics, and military organization would have been of immense value to a more united people. But the crises and alarms that divided Europe prevented the pope, or anyone else, from making preparations to face a fresh Mongol invasion. The only action that the pope thought necessary

Above: Kuyuk Khan, who was crowned during Carpini's visit. The khan declined the monk's invitation to become a Christian and gave him a letter for the pope, requesting him to journey east and pay Kuyuk homage.

was to send a further mission to the court of the Great Khan.

This party, under a Dominican friar called Ascelin, or Anselm, did not travel Carpini's route but relived many of his experiences—nightmare travel, scant food, insults, delays. Ascelin had been ordered to visit the camp of the Mongol army in Persia and demand cessation of hostilities against Christendom. He seems to have been a poor diplomat. After a harsh reception, probably justified by his own rudeness, at the camp to the west of the Caspian Sea, he was

Right: the seal of Kuyuk Khan. The inscription reads: 'In the power of Eternal Heaven, the order of the oceanic Khan of the people of the Great Mongols. The conquered people must respect it and fear them.'

saved from execution only by an envoy of the Great Khan himself. In 1248, Ascelin was sent home with a letter to the pope, similar to the one Carpini had carried, but written by Baiju Noyan, a Mongol khan of Asia Minor. Ascelin was accompanied on the homeward path by two Mongol envoys who were received at the papal court of Innocent IV.

Pope Innocent's missions to the Mongol court all failed in their aim of persuading the khan to give up the idea of making further conquests in the West. But, apart from the easternmost countries, Europe was never invaded by the Mongols. There can be little doubt that only the imperial Mongol deaths and the resulting struggle for succession saved western Europe from Mongol rampages during these critical years.

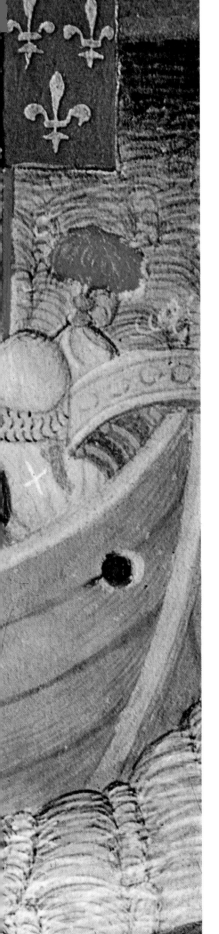

The Travels of William of Rubruck 7

In the mid-1200's, Europe waited, trembling, in fear of a Mongol attack. Meanwhile, King Louis IX of France, later canonized (made a saint) because of his devout and saintly life, was preparing a Crusade to Palestine. Among Louis' following was a certain Franciscan friar called William. He was born in 1215, in the village of Rubruck in Flanders, and is generally referred to simply as Rubruck. He would almost certainly have heard from Carpini's own lips a full account of that epoch-making journey to Mongolia and back. Perhaps it was Carpini's story that first fired Rubruck with the idea of making the journey himself.

If so, this ambition must have been boosted in 1248, when Louis' party, including Rubruck as envoy, arrived in Cyprus and was met by a messenger from Djagatai, the Mongol commander in the area of what is now Iran and southern Russia. The message he carried was highly complimentary to Louis, and it offered an alliance against the Moslems in Palestine. The timely arrival of this well-informed envoy shows how very competent the Mongol intelligence network in Europe was at that time. Louis sent a favorable reply to Djagatai and he also sent a mission to the Great Khan. He did not yet know that Kuyuk was dead.

This mission, under Friar Andrew of Longumel, who had been Louis' interpreter, set out in February, 1249, with letters and a rich assortment of gifts. Unfortunately, only second-hand accounts of their journey survive, and their route is known only from passing references in Rubruck's later account. In the meantime, Louis'

Left: King Louis IX (Saint Louis) setting out in 1248, on the first of his two Crusades. Louis was taken prisoner on his first Crusade and died of plague during the second.

Right: William of Rubruck, the Franciscan friar and envoy of King Louis who trekked by covered wagon and on horseback to Karakoram, the court of Mangu Khan, and back to Europe—a round trip of about 11,000 miles.

Left: this illuminated letter from a medieval manuscript shows (above) Rubruck and a companion before King Louis, and (below) the two travelers setting out on their journey.

Below: Saint Sophia, in Istanbul, Turkey. Built in the 500's as a Christian cathedral, the minarets were added much later when the Turks converted it to a mosque. When Rubruck visited the city, Saint Sophia was still a Christian church.

Crusade was going disastrously. He had been defeated in Egypt, captured, and ransomed, when Friar Andrew returned with this message from the empress regent: "A good thing is peace; for in a land of peace those that go upon four legs eat grass peaceably. Those that go on two legs work the earth whose fruits come laboriously . . . these things we admonish you for your best advice; for you can have no peace except from us; the same could be told you by such and such kings . . . and all whom we have put to the sword. We advise you that if you will send us some of your gold and your silver, you will retain our friendship and if you do not do it, we will destroy you and your race as we have destroyed those mentioned above."

Andrew, though he penetrated only to the western edge of the Mongol heartland, brought back a wealth of information about the Mongols—and some misinformation, including rumors that the Mongol chief Sartach, son of the great Batu of the Golden Horde, had been converted to Christianity. If Rubruck had had no ambition to go east before, this must surely have aroused his interest. The chance of converting, as he thought, more of the Mongols to Christianity was one that no devout Christian could neglect.

The next European envoy to the Mongols was Philip de Toucy, a knight, who, together with some brother knights, had been sent on a mission to the Golden Horde by Baldwin II, Emperor of Constantinople, who maintained close ties with Louis IX—Saint Louis—of France. One of De Toucy's party not only married a Russian princess, but also visited the imperial Mongol camp near Karakoram. Rubruck, with the other members of Louis' court,

90

Above: one of the five existing manuscripts of the journey of William of Rubruck, dating from the 1300's. As a record of Mongolian life and customs, it is as important as the later narrative of Marco Polo.

would have met and talked to all these travelers. From their accounts, a great deal was learned about the Mongols.

De Toucy's party stayed with Louis for about a year, so Rubruck had ample time to ask advice and plan his route. De Toucy's advice determined him to travel by way of Russia instead of by the Middle East and Iran, as Andrew had done. Louis, still smarting from the empress regent's high-handed letter, would not give the mission his official seal, but he gave individual members of the party some money, a few gifts for the rulers they would meet on their journey, and letters of reference and commendation.

In the spring of 1252, Rubruck's party, accompanying De Toucy's men on their way back to Baldwin, reached Constantinople. There Rubruck stayed until May 7, 1253, when he and his companions started on their 27-month round trip to Karakoram. In contrast to the other missions from the West, this one was purely religious in character. The members of the party were careful always to insist that they were not ambassadors but men of religion, and

that their sole concern was to teach and spread the word of God.

In some ways Rubruck's journey was easier than Carpini's. The unknown was not quite as unknown as it had been eight years before. Carpini had blazed the trail, and other envoys had endorsed his account of the conditions and peoples the traveler could expect to meet. Rubruck was able to profit by their experiences and equip his party with regard to their advice. Moreover, he was starting his journey from eastern, not western, Europe, and so, before leaving, he could have the letters he took with him translated into various central Asian languages. He too was a fat and heavy man, but he was younger and healthier than Carpini had been. Nonetheless Rubruck's achievements were highly creditable. Fortunately, the story of his adventures, written by his own hand, has come down to us intact. A much more personal account than Carpini's business-like dossier of events, it is full of anecdotes and intimate observations.

From Constantinople, Rubruck and his companions traveled by sea to Soldaria (now Sudak), then a great merchant port in the

Above: a monastery near the site of the khan's ancient palace at Karakoram. Founded by Genghis Khan in 1220, the Mongol capital was not impressive by European standards. In 1264, Kublai Khan moved his capital to Cambaluc (later known as Peking).

Crimea, and terminus of the land route to Russia and Asia. Taking to the land, they set off with six oxcarts and made contact with the first Mongols within three days. Making much slower progress than Carpini had done due to the cumbersome covered wagons, the party followed a more northerly route through central Asia than that taken by the Franciscans seven years before. Rubruck corrected Carpini's mistake about the true mouths of the Ural and Volga rivers. He also realized that the Caspian is an inland sea, not, as Carpini had thought, a gulf connected to the Mediterranean and Black seas.

Like Carpini, Rubruck visited Batu at his camp on the Volga, and was there directed to make for the court of the Great Khan. Touching on Carpini's route again, Rubruck and his party underwent the same kinds of hardships as the earlier mission had had to withstand. But even throughout this taxing spell, Rubruck took the time to

write full details of the journey, the countryside, and the different tribes and animals he saw on the way. A skilled linguist, he used his knowledge and observation to sort out the origins of a number of races and tribes. For instance, Rubruck noted the affinity among Russians, Poles, Slavs, and Bohemians, and he traced their descent back to a common origin. He also gave the first description, and it is nearly accurate, of Chinese writing—comparing it with Tibetan, Arabic, and other scripts. Then he described the scattered Christian communities he came across. Most of these had been converted to the Nestorian belief by Arab and Persian merchants. Nestorians were members of a heretical sect which had been prominent in the A.D. 400's. They did not recognize Mary as the mother of God, and believed Jesus Christ to have distinct divine and human persons. Rubruck also gave an account of Buddhism, and was the first European to identify Cathay as the home of silk traders known to Europe as "Seres, from whom are brought most excellent stuffes of silk."

On December 27, 1253, the traveling friars reached the encampment of the new Great Khan, Mangu, another grandson of Genghis Khan. Singing a Latin hymn, Rubruck and his men entered Mangu's dwelling. "The house was all covered inside with a cloth of gold . . . Mangu was seated on a couch and was dressed in a skin spotted and glossy, like a seal's skin. He is a little man, of medium height, aged 45 years . . . he appeared to me to be intoxicated." The friars' interpreter soon also began to suffer from the effects of too much

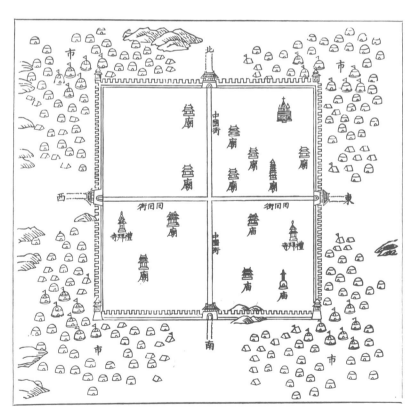

Right: plan of Karakoram, showing the royal palace, mosques, shrines, and, improbably, churches. The outer walls are surrounded by nomad tents.

wine, and so after giving formal greetings, the Europeans retired. A miserable hut was assigned for their use, but the khan graciously invited the priests to stay at his camp for two months, until the end of the great cold. During these months, it was so cold that Rubruck says the tips of his toes froze, and he could no longer go barefoot as was his custom. He must have been a hardy soul, however, for during this spell of very cold weather, the Mongols presented the other friar in Rubruck's party, and the interpreter, with cloaks, trousers, and shoes, all made of sheepskin. But Rubruck refused them, saying a fur cloak Batu had given him was enough.

When the two months were up, Rubruck accompanied Mangu to his capital and gave Europe its first account of that city: "You must know that, exclusive of the palace of the Khan, Karakoram is not as big as the village of Saint Denis [a small French provincial village], and the monastery of Saint Denis is 10 times larger than the palace."

Men of almost every race and religion met at the Great Khan's capital, and Rubruck recorded descriptions of many of them in his journal. He also wrote some highly colorful accounts of the endless drinking parties, which were a common form of entertainment among all nationalities.

One year after leaving Batu's camp, Rubruck and his companions passed through it again on their way home. They carried with them a letter from Mangu to King Louis. "The commandments of the eternal God are what we impart to you . . . if you understand it and shall not give heed to it nor believe it, saying: 'Our country is far off, our mountains are strong, our sea is wide' and in this belief you make war against us, you shall find out what we can do."

In 1255, they reached Christian soil again and Rubruck returned to the monastery of his order to send a report of his travels, and the not very encouraging message from the khan, to King Louis at Acre ('Akko). Religious missions to Mongolia then ceased for more than 30 years.

Happily for Christendom, the Mongols now turned their attentions again to the Islamic countries. At the very time when Rubruck was in Karakoram, the Great Khan and his brother had been planning attacks on two of the leaders of the Moslem world, the Caliph of Baghdad and the Grand Master of the Ismailis, and these they proceeded to put into action. In 1258, Mangu died, and power passed to his brother Kublai.

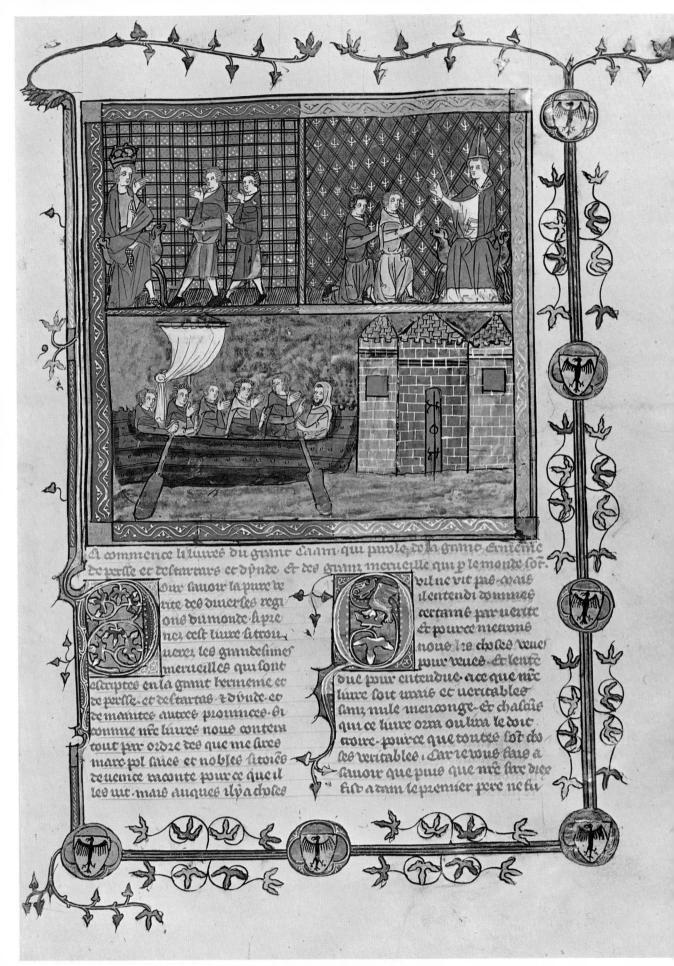

Cy commence li liures du grant caaim qui parole de la grant éuiente
de perse et destartars et dynte. et des grant merueille qui p̄ lemonde sōt.

Our sauoir la pure ne
rite des diuerses regi
ons du monde si pre
nez cest liure sitrou
uerez les grandesimes
merueilles qui sont
escriptes enla grant bermenie et
de perse. et destartas ꝫ dynde. co
de maintes autres prouinces. si
comme nre liures nous contera
tout par ordre des que me sires
marc pol saiues et nobles sitoires
de uenice raconte pour ce que il
les uit mais auques ily a choses

uil ne uit pas. mais
il entendi dommes
certains par uertte
ꝫ pource metrons
nous les choses ueues
pour ueues. ꝫ lentē
due pour entendue. cicc que nre
liure soit urais et ueritables
sanz nulle mensonge. et chascun
qui ce liure orra ou lira le doit
croire. pource que toutes sōt cho
ses ueritables. car ie uous fais a
sauoir que puis que nre sire dieu
fist adam le premier pere ne fu

Merchant Travelers

8

Left: a beautiful illumination, from a medieval manuscript, of Nicolò and Maffeo Polo setting out on their journey to the Orient. At top left, they are seen arriving in Constantinople. On the right, they are received there by the Emperor of Constantinople, Baldwin. Below: they and their companions row into a Black Sea port.

Most of the early European journeys to Asia were undertaken by men of God—missionaries seeking converts among the heathen, or envoys from the Christian pope. In the late 1200's, they were succeeded by merchants, who became the first non-Asians known to have crossed Asia from the Mediterranean Sea to the Pacific Ocean. The first detailed account of Europeans visiting the Far East concerns two merchants from Venice—Nicolò and Maffeo Polo.

The Venetian republic was at that time one of the richest and most powerful of the city-states into which the north of Italy was divided. Its merchants specialized in the valuable trade between Europe and the Middle East. Their ships sailed regularly to the ports of the eastern Mediterranean, and even as far as the Black Sea, carrying European products such as cloth on the outward journey and Oriental luxury goods and spices on the homeward trip. To secure and protect these profitable trade routes, Venice had gained possession of a number of islands, including Crete, and part of the Greek mainland. Venetian merchants were accustomed to dealing with Eastern traders, and many of them could speak the principal languages of the Middle East.

In 1260, Kublai, the brother of Mangu Khan, became Great Khan of the vast Mongol Empire. A man of immense vision, with an

Right: this Venetian ship, worked in jewels and enamels, is part of the priceless *Pala d'Oro*, the great altar screen in Venice's St. Mark's basilica. In the Polos' time, sailing ships carried Venetian traders to all parts of the Mediterranean and the Black Sea.

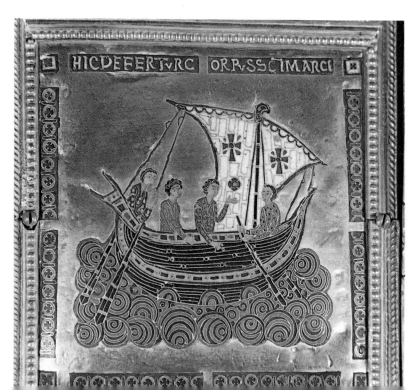

Right: a silk moth. Silk was first made in China and was an important export commodity from the beginning of the Christian era. It was taken to the Middle East by the overland caravan route and by sea. Only during the reign of Kublai Khan were Europeans first able to travel directly to China and engage in the silk trade.

outstanding talent for administration, Kublai was in many ways as rare a person as his grandfather, Genghis, had been. During his reign the Mongol Empire included the whole of China (then generally known as Cathay), Korea, and Tibet, as well as parts of Indochina and Burma. Other states outside this area, except Japan which he was never able to conquer, sent him tribute every year. Kublai ran the administrative machine of his empire with energy, compassion, and a sense of purpose. Because huge distances separated the parts of his empire, he radically reformed his administration along Chinese lines then moved his capital from Karakoram to a city he called Cambaluc. This city in China was later called Peking.

During the reign of Kublai Khan, the Mongols gave up their destructive warlike activities, and a period of prosperity and tolerance began throughout their empire. The road system, with its

Below: when the Polos set out on their first journey across Asia in 1260, their home city-state of Venice had built up an important eastward-looking commercial empire in the Mediterranean. This map shows the extent of that empire and its trading routes in 1250. By 1450, this complex would make Venice the strongest sea power in the Christian world.

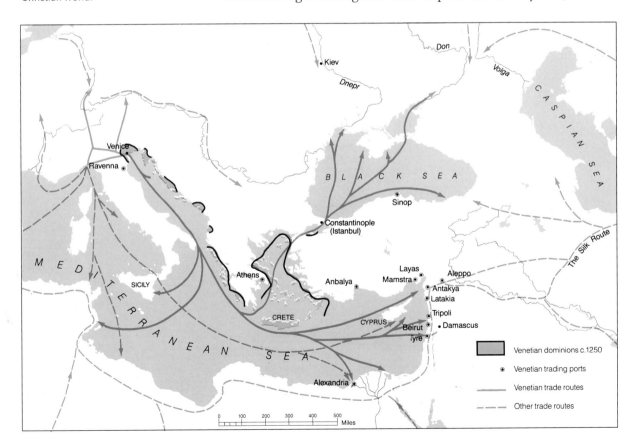

inns and post horses, was already efficient in the time of Carpini and Rubruck. Now it was so well organized that anyone, Mongol or foreigner, could travel easily from Europe to the empire's easternmost outpost. The roads were good. In most places they were covered with earth, suitable for riders, elsewhere they were paved for wheeled traffic. Trees marked the borders of the roads in fertile areas, and in desert regions there was a line of white stones along each side. The roads were also safe. "A maiden bearing a nugget of gold," it was said, "could walk these roads alone and unmolested." Merchants of many nations began to use the roads, and direct trade took place between Europe and China for the first time.

In Roman times, there had been regular comings and goings along the Silk Roads, the original caravan routes from eastern China to the West. However, few if any Europeans traveled the distance to China. The Moslem conquests in Asia in the 600's disturbed communications between East and West. As a result, knowledge of the East grew dim in European memory. But six-and-a-half centuries later, Kublai Khan received and welcomed merchants from the West and, for a short time, the East was accessible to Europeans.

In, or shortly after, 1255, while Rubruck was hastening back to Europe, Nicolò and Maffeo Polo set out for Constantinople on a trading trip. They remained in Constantinople for several years then sailed on to the port of Sudak in the Crimea where their brother, Marco Polo the elder, was a leading member of the resident Venetian

Above: under the Great Khan, most Mongols were pagans, worshiping the spirit forces in winds, forests, and mountains. These figures are demons, part-human, part-animal. Despite the later arrival of Buddhism and, in more recent times, Communism, many Mongolian peasants remain faithful to the old pagan beliefs and customs.

Above: the ancient city of Bukhara, in Uzbekistan, U.S.S.R., was sacked by the warriors of Genghis Khan. By the time the Polo brothers visited the city, it had been rebuilt. They were so impressed with Bukhara that they stayed there for three years.

trading community. The Polos carried jewels with them instead of money or goods, because jewels were lighter, easier to carry, and easier to conceal. In Sudak, business seems to have been slack and the brothers had the idea of opening up a trading route to Russia—to Sarai (then a city on the lower Volga, northwest of Astrakhan), where Barka, brother of the now-dead Batu and new Khan of the Golden Horde, had set up his capital. For centuries Christian merchants from Italy had been trading profitably with their spiritual enemies—Moslems, Jews, and other *infidels* (unbelievers). Trade with the "Tartar devils," so recently the terror of the West, came just as naturally.

Leaving Marco in Sudak, Nicolò and Maffeo went to Sarai, where their venture was a great success. The Polos presented all their valuable jewels to Barka, and he gave them goods of twice the value in return. The Polos stayed at his court for a year, a period about which very little is known. Then, just as they intended to start back to the Crimea, Barka went to war with the khan whose lands lay to the south and west of Sarai. Bitter fighting made the route by which the Polos had come too dangerous to travel.

Nicolò and Maffeo decided to try to find a roundabout way home, and set off eastward. From Bolgar, at the northern limit of Mongol dominions, they crossed the Volga and then traveled to Bukhara, chief city of another of the subsidiary khans, Djagatai. The Polos remained for three years at his court, and thought Bukhara the "finest city in the whole of Persia" and very good for business. Then, one day in 1265, Mongol envoys from the west of Iran came through Bukhara on their way to Cambaluc. The envoys said that Kublai was most anxious to meet Westerners, and invited the Polos to make the long journey to China with them.

Perhaps in the spirit of adventure, perhaps in the hope of increasing trade, the two Polos took up the invitation, and joined the Mongol caravan. They traveled eastward for about a year, with none of the haste but some of the discomfort the religious travelers had put up with. On the way, they stopped at Samarkand, now in Uzbekistan, which Marco later described as "a very great and noble city . . . it has splendid gardens and a plain full of all the fruits one could possibly desire." Then they progressed along the northern branch of the Silk Road to join the southern branch at Tunhwang in north central China. From Tunhwang the Polos and their escorts went eastward to the Yellow River (now the Hwang Ho) and then on to Peking, once the center of ancient China, at that time (under the name of Cambaluc) capital of the Mongol Empire.

Kublai Khan received the Venetians with courtesy. He was interested in these foreigners and questioned them closely on Western customs and affairs. The brothers had by now lived in Mongol states for several years, long enough to become fluent in Asian languages. Their answers impressed and pleased the Great Khan. He determined to send them, with one of his own noblemen,

Below: a detail from the Catalan Atlas of 1375, showing the brothers Polo traveling by camel caravan.

as his envoys to the pope. They were to request the pope to send Kublai 100 men "skilled in the seven arts," and having a deep knowledge of Christianity, to argue and demonstrate the superiority of their religion before the court in Cambaluc. Kublai also asked for some of the oil from the lamp over Christ's sepulcher in Jerusalem. Then he presented the Venetians with a golden tablet, a kind of passport to comfort on their journey back. The tablet was a 15-inch gold strip with an inscription on it to the glory of the khan of khans. At any point within the Mongol Empire the tablet guaranteed the traveler food, lodgings, fresh horses, and an escort.

The Mongol nobleman fell ill early on the journey back and returned to Cambaluc. Nicolò and Maffeo continued on their own, not reaching Acre in northern Palestine until three years later. Little is known of their route, and why they took so long. Presumably they stopped for long intervals to trade at places on the way. From Acre, the Polos embarked directly for Venice. There Nicolò learned that the wife he had left behind some 14 years earlier had long since died. His son Marco, who had been a baby when he left, was now a bright and strapping 15-year-old.

It was a bad time to bring Kublai's request back to Europe. Pope Clement IV had died in 1268, and a long quarrel was going on about his successor. The Polos waited impatiently for more than two years, daily hoping for the appointment of a pope who would grant Kublai's request. By 1271, their patience had run out. Fearing that the trading trail they had blazed would close up if they delayed any longer, the brothers left for Acre again, this time taking young Marco with them. At Acre they met the papal legate, Tebaldo Visconti, and explained the situation to him. Visconti saw at once the golden chance their contact with China presented to Christendom and agreed that the Polos ought to keep open the line to Cambaluc. But he could give them no official papal reply until there was a pope to authorize it.

Left: Kublai Khan handing the golden tablet to the Polo brothers at his new capital of Cambaluc. The Polos left no written record of their time there.

The Polos went to Jerusalem to get the holy oil that Kublai had asked for. Then they set off again for Cambaluc. They had only reached Layas, a port in the northeast corner of the Mediterranean, when they heard that a new pope had been elected and they were to return to Acre. The new pope was none other than Tebaldo Visconti, who assumed the title of Pope Gregory X. He was still at Acre. He gave the Polos full ambassadorial status and many fine presents, including valuable crystals, for the khan. The church could neither muster nor spare the 100 learned theologians Kublai Khan had asked for—especially at such short notice. Instead the pope sent along two Dominican friars, Friar Nicholas of Vicenza and Friar William of Tripoli, to help convert the Chinese and Mongols. The two friars got no farther than Layas. There, scared by the fighting then going on between Egyptians and Armenians, they handed all their privileges, papers, and letters over to the Polos and made for home. At a time when Kublai and the Mongols were open to conversion, who knows what a lost opportunity their defection may have caused to the Christian church?

Tebaldo Visconti had become acquainted in Acre with Prince Edward, later Edward I of England. In the English prince's retinue at that time was a young romance writer called Rusticello. He had probably heard of and may have met the three Venetians, whose most exciting adventures were then beginning. Their tale, entitled

Above: the port of Acre, in Israel. Acre dates back 3,500 years. In the Middle Ages, it was the gateway to the East. Nicolò and Maffeo Polo sailed from there to Venice in 1269, and returned two years later with young Marco Polo, at the beginning of their second journey to the East.

Right: title page of the first printed edition in 1477, of *The Book of Marco Polo*. There are over 140 known manuscripts of the book, including handwritten versions of the 1300's.

Left: Asia and eastern Europe, showing the vast distances and formidable terrain that the early European travelers, missionaries, and merchants braved in their amazing journeys to the East.

Below: an illustration from a medieval French manuscript of *The Book of Marco Polo*, showing travelers in Armenia, a region in southwestern Asia.

The Book of Marco Polo, he was to set down in a Genoese prison which he shared with Marco Polo the younger over 25 years later.

In a way, Rusticello's collaboration mars the early part of Marco's story, which reads much more like a romantic fable than a real journey. Marco Polo's main contribution to the joint work was probably the rather dull commercial geography which is typical of long sections of the book. For instance: "Southwest of the Black Sea, the region of Mount Ararat [Greater Armenia] is a large province. Near the entrance to it stands a city called Erzincan, in which is made the best buckram in the world and countless other crafts are practiced." Rusticello, like the princes, bishops, knights, and merchants who read his words or listened to his tales, already knew the Middle East fairly well and so he included at this stage a series of lengthy passages repeating well-known Middle East legends, no doubt intended to make the work more exciting.

For the later and greater parts of this amazing journey, when the Polos had passed out of the reasonably familiar Middle East into lands he knew nothing about, Rusticello had to rely on Marco Polo's memories. From that point the story is richer, more detailed, and more interestingly told.

Ci apres comence le liure de marc pol des merueilles dou se la grant et dit
le la maiour ermeingne. Et des diuerses regions du monde
Pur sauoir la pure verite de diuerses regions du mon
de. Si prenes ce liure cy et le faittes lire. si y trouueres les
grandismes merueilles qui y sont escriptes. De la grãt
ermenie. et de perse. et des tartars et dinde et de main
tes autres prouinces. si comme nre liure comptera p
ordres apertement. de quoy messire marc pol. sages et
nobles citoiens de venise mcompte pour ce que il le

The Venetians Return
9

Left: a page from an illuminated
medieval manuscript, showing the
Polos leaving on their second journey
to the court of the Great Khan.

The three Polos, having taken their leave of the timid friars, set off again from Layas in 1271, to make their way to Hormuz at the southeastern corner of the Persian Gulf. Traveling about 20 miles a day along a wide, fertile plain set between arid mountains, the Polos reached Kermān in southeast Iran without undue incident. Here the caravan roads ran north and south. The Venetians took the south road to Hormuz, about 200 miles away. Seven days after leaving Kermān, there was a sharp climb up into a 10,000-foot-high pass where they were exposed to extreme cold and the possibility of being maimed by frostbite. Surviving the dangers without harm, the travelers then had to make their way down the long descent to a hot, densely populated plain, infested with marauding bandits. A group of these raiders attacked the Polos, who had a very narrow escape, doubtless one of many on the early part of their journey. Six days' march took them on to the well-watered, fruitful plain leading to Hormuz itself.

Hormuz was the terminus of the sea routes from India and China. It was then centered on an island just off the coast, although within the next 200 years it was moved to the mainland. Each week, ships brought in spices, precious stones, pearls, gold, silks, elephants' tusks, and other exotic wares. In spite of the richness of its trade, Marco found Hormuz an extremely unattractive place. He hated

Right: the Polos planned to travel
by sea from Hormuz, a port on the
Persian Gulf. They changed their minds
when they saw the rickety ships
intended to transport them across the
Indian Ocean. In this picture, travelers
are trying to board a boat already carrying a camel, a horse, and an elephant!

Above: a nomad family in Iran (Persia). The Polos' traveled through Iran and across the central plateau to what is today Afghanistan. The country they passed through was probably very like that seen here.

its hot, dry climate, so different from the plains behind it, and recounts the terrifying tale of how a whole army was once destroyed there by the burning heat and the suffocating dust-laden wind from the desert.

At this stage of their journey, Maffeo, Nicolò, and Marco decided to go the whole way to the court of the khan by land. They had thought of going by sea from Hormuz, but changed their minds after their first sight of the flimsy, unseaworthy-looking boats they would have sailed in.

With their retinue, the Polos went north again from the coast to Kermān, along a more easterly route up a path studded with many "hot baths"—sulphur springs. Kermān was at the southeastern edge of a great desert land, 100 miles of huge gravel slopes and sand hills with only occasional salt lakes to relieve the dryness. Grim reminders of the perils the desert held for the unlucky traveler were ever present in the animal skulls and skeletons which lay scattered all over the ground. Marco's own description of this part of the journey gives a very clear picture: "On leaving the city of Kermān one has seven days of most wearisome riding and I will tell you why. During the first three days one finds no water, or practically none, and what one does find is brackish and as green as meadow grass, and so bitter that no one could possibly drink it . . . On the fourth day one reaches a fresh-water river flowing underground . . . at the end of these seven days one finds the city of Cobinah". This city no longer exists, but was probably 100 miles north of Kermān.

After several days more of arduous desert travel, the Venetians reached the welcome, temperate climate of Tunocain in northeast Iran. The townsmen of Tunocain told Marco many tales about a person known as the "Old Man of the Mountain," one of the most amazing of legendary Asian rulers. The Old Man lived in a great castle south of the Caspian Sea. He was head of a heretical Islamic sect founded in the 1000's, and his subjects believed him to be a prophet of God. The Old Man had constructed near his castle a garden, representing paradise, "running with conduits of wine and milk and honey and water, and full of lovely women for the delectation of its inmates."

The Old Man drugged young men among his followers with hashish—from which comes their title of *hash-shashin* (hemp-eaters) or Assassins—and had them conveyed to the garden to enjoy its pleasures. They were then drugged again and taken out of it.

Right: the garden-like paradise of the Old Man of the Mountain, with its lovely inmates. The Old Man is seen outside his castle, showing an unsuspecting, presumably drugged, young guest some of the garden's delights. *(Bodleian Library, Oxford. MS. Bodley 264, fol. 226.)*

Above: a village in modern Afghanistan, near the Silk Road, with typical dome-shaped houses. Merchant caravans passed regularly through this rugged country, as did the Mongol warriors from the East. The Polos traveled through the Hindu Kush and the Pamirs —the so-called "roof of the world."

Believing that they had been in paradise itself, the Assassins would do anything the Old Man ordered them to do, exposing themselves recklessly to any danger, even loss of life, in order to get back into "paradise." As a result, the Old Man was able to get rid of his enemies by commanding the Assassins to murder anyone he wanted. When the Mongols conquered the Persian area of central Asia, they came up against the Old Man, and, after a long struggle, finally eradicated him and his sect in 1256, 16 years before Marco's visit to Tunocain. Though some of the stories about the Old Man are only legends, they had a basis of truth. Such murders—*assassinations*—had taken place during the reigns of certain Moslem rulers in the area from the 1000's on. And the uses of hashish had certainly been exploited by these leaders.

Leaving Tunocain, the Polos journeyed eastward toward the fertile valley of the Hari River. In his story of this part of the travels, Marco mentions the city of Balkh, which marked the eastern boundary of the Ilkhanate of Persia. This city, still great and noble in the late 1200's, had, he says, been even more magnificent in earlier times but "the Tartars and other peoples have ravaged and destroyed it." In the classical age, Balkh had been a symbol of the power and extent of Alexander the Great's empire, and was reputed to be

the location of the conqueror's marriage to a Persian princess. In the Polos' time it still marked a well-known junction of trade routes. From Balkh, roads ran due north to Samarkand, northwest to Bukhara, southeast to Kabul (today the capital of Afghanistan), and the mountain province of Peshāwar, and east to Kashgar and Yarkand. On their previous visit to Cathay, the elder Polos had gone east from Bukhara. This time, with Marco, they were on a different route. At Balkh they continued on the more direct and shorter, but more difficult southerly route.

This path lay east through the mountain ranges of the Hindu Kush and the Pamirs, known as the *roof of the world*. It was the greatest undertaking the travelers had yet attempted. The first sections of the march were taxing but not too difficult. On a plateau of the Hindu Kush, "after a hard day's work to get to the top," the Polos reached a wide grassy plain with flowering trees and trout-filled streams. This "tableland" was regarded by valley dwellers in the locality almost as a health resort. Marco had been ill for about a year, but recovered "at once" on the plateau. It is not clear from his writings how long had elapsed since the start of the Polos' journey, but at about this time, perhaps because of Marco's ill-health, the travelers stopped and rested for several months.

Above: an execution in Afghanistan. This illumination comes from *Les Livres Merveilles,* a medieval French manuscript containing Polo's *Book*.

Below: a magnificently horned wild sheep of the Pamir plateau, named *Ovis poli* after Marco Polo.

From the plateau, the Polos went up into higher mountains, traveling for 12 days northeastward along the great Oxus River (the Amu-Darya). Still going northeast, they climbed steeply for three more days to reach "the highest place in the world." On this plateau, between 13,000 and 15,000 feet above sea level with peaks of 19,000 feet or more in view, Marco Polo saw the wild sheep with curved horns $4\frac{1}{2}$ feet long which are today called *Ovis poli* after him. Here, too, Marco comments on the bitter coldness of the weather and the difficulty that he and his companions experienced in cooking their food. "No birds fly here because of the height and the cold. And I assure you that, because of this great cold, fire here is not so bright nor of the same color as elsewhere, and food does not cook well." He did not know that with increased altitude and decreased atmospheric pressure, water boils at a lower temperature, and the food in it does not cook as quickly as when water boils at 100°C.

Leaving the Pamirs thankfully behind, the Polos went down by the side of the Yaman-yar River to the pleasant city of Kashgar, chief town of the vast plain of east Turkestan, now the region of Sinkiang, part of the People's Republic of China. Kashgar, an oasis indeed after the barren treeless mountains, had "splendid gardens and vineyards and fine farms," and its people lived "contentedly by trade and handicrafts."

To the east of Kashgar lies the vast, sandy desert of Taklamakan. Annual rainfall over the whole area is negligible and the oases around the edges depend on the few rivers and water holes. Here is Marco's view of a Turkestan desert:

"All this province is a tract of sand . . . when it happens that an army passes through the country, if it is a hostile one, the people take flight with their wives and children and their beasts, two or three days into the sandy wastes, to places where they know that there is water and they can live with their beasts. And I assure you that no one can tell which way they have gone because the wind covers their tracks with sand so that there is nothing to show where they have been, but the country looks as if it had never been traversed by man or beast." When what Marco calls "friendly" armies passed by, the inhabitants would merely drive their animals into the wastes so that the soldiers could not seize and eat them. When the locals harvested their meager supplies of grain, they stored them in caves in the desert, far from human habitation and passing armies, and then

took back home whatever rations they required month by month.

The Polos skirted the desert's western edges to Yarkand, in present-day Sinkiang, where, Marco Polo notes, "they mostly have goiters [a swelling of the thyroid gland in the neck, usually caused by lack of iodine in the diet]." Travelers in the present century have confirmed that this is still the case, one indication that many things in these remote regions have changed very little since Marco Polo's time.

For each of the principal oases on the caravan route through the sands of Sinkiang, Marco Polo gives a condensed guide to merchants concerning its size, trade, local products, and customs. All the cities he mentions at this stage of the journey had once been famous as stopping places on the southern branch of the Silk Road. Forgotten and neglected for centuries, they were no longer prosperous. As can be seen from Marco's account, most had been attacked and overrun several times by successive nomad bands before the Mongols came to power. Nonetheless, although the roads had not been reopened long enough to regain very much of their past prosperity, certain prized commodities were still to be found in the towns along this part of the road. Among these were coveted precious stones, including jade, and various unusual products, such as asbestos.

When the Polos reached the oasis called Lop, near Lake Lop Nor, after five days' exhausting trek across the sand, they were nearing the edge of the great Gobi, the most terrifying desert of all. Here "travelers take a week's rest in order to refresh themselves and their

animals, they take food for a month for man and beast . . . this desert is reported to be so long that it would take a year to go from end to end and at the narrowest point it takes a month to cross it. It consists entirely of mountains and sand and valleys. There is nothing to eat . . . but after traveling a day and a night in winter you find drinking water . . . all the way through the desert you must go for a day and a night before you find water . . . beasts and birds there are none, because they find nothing to eat." Marco then goes on to tell of the strange tricks the desert can play upon lonely travelers— mirages, phantom sounds, ghostly marauders, and spirit voices that terrify or lure men to their destruction in the empty wastes.

About this point in the journey, the youngest Polo may more than once have doubted his elders' wisdom in embarking on such a route. Not counting detours, the three men and their attendants had traveled some 2,500 miles since setting out from Hormuz—almost the whole way through deserts and high mountains. What wares could possibly justify trade along so difficult and hazardous a route?

Above: camels in the Gobi Desert. The total area of the desert is about 500,000 square miles, but despite Marco Polo's daunting description, only certain parts consist solely of sand. Much of it is rocky, with sparse vegetation and occasional grass-land, watered by seasonal streams.

Left: sets of Chinese gold earrings of the Mongol period. Such ornaments would have been brought back to Europe by the merchants who traveled by the Asian caravan routes or by sea.

Right: shipping on the River Caramoran, the Mongol name for China's Hwang Ho River, fortified castles, and a traveler and packhorse approaching an inn. Marco Polo traveled along lengthy stretches of this river, bustling with trade, while traveling in China. *(Bodleian Library, Oxford. MS. Bodley 264, fol. 245 v.)*

If Marco Polo ever did entertain such doubts, he was quite right to do so. We have no record that any European trader ever trod this part of the Polos' path to Cathay again by way of regular business, although such goods as silk, cotton, iron, leather, and gems did pass from merchant to merchant all the way along it from Cathay without duty or hindrance. Some of the goods also found their way to the Middle East and so to Europe. Certainly, after the Polos eventually returned to Venice, they sent no caravans back along the route they had taken, nor did they encourage others to do so. The route favored by later traders was always the more northerly one taken by the two elder Polos on their first visit.

Any hope of easy trade must have dwindled further in Marco's mind as he and his companions made their way from water hole to water hole along the fringes of the great Gobi. Nevertheless, Marco must have had cause to return to this region at least once during his years in the service of Kublai Khan, because he describes places well away from the route the Polos took through Sinkiang at this time. Among those he writes of are Karakoram, 40 days' march away (in the late 1200's, no longer the Mongol capital), and the Turfan Depression, where one can stand in a plain that dips to 505 feet below sea level and look north to where the Bogdo Ola Mountains rise to almost 18,000 feet above it.

On this first journey, after 30 days' march from the last oasis, Marco, Nicolò, and Maffeo Polo reached the city called Tunhwang in Cathay, near the junction of the north and south branches of the Silk Road. Nicolò and Maffeo had already been there on their previous journey. In the 1900's, a scholar and archaeologist working at

Above: the Siberian Mekriti tribe was described by Marco Polo as a savage people who hunted and rode on reindeer. Strange though they may have appeared to Europeans, they can hardly have been quite as grotesque as this painting suggests.

the site of the Caves of the Thousand Buddhas, about eight miles from Tunhwang itself, found a huge hoard of manuscripts, paintings, embroideries, and figurines dating from the A.D. 400's to 900's. It is not known whether Marco visited these caves, but he describes Tunhwang as having "abbeys and monasteries all of which are full of all kinds of idols, to which they [the inhabitants of the region] offer great sacrifices and pay great honor and worship." He also describes the Buddhist practice of cremating the dead, and explains how paper models of men, camels, and horses were burned beside the corpse, in the hope that they would be of use to the deceased person in the life after death.

From Tunhwang, the Polo's caravan traveled for 10 days, first northeast, then south to Suchow (Kiuchuan) and finally to Kanchow (Changyeh), where the Polos remained for about a year. From Kanchow they proceeded to Liangchow. This journey gives rise to a curious feature of this section of *The Book of Marco Polo*. In the Polo's day the Great Wall of China ran unbroken from the vicinity of Liangchow to the sea east of Cambaluc. But although the caravan must have followed beside, if not actually ridden upon the wall for some of the way from Liangchow, which is on its extremity, Marco never once mentions its existence.

Leaving Liangchow, the Venetians pushed east again, going toward the Hwang Ho and away from the usual caravan route. They made "eight more stages to the east. . . ." Marco says the route then lay through the "principal seat of Prester John . . . whose descendants still live there . . . in that part that in our country is known as Gog and Magog, [according to the New Testament, two nations that make war on the kingdom of Christ]." This mistaken reference in *The Book of Marco Polo* to the kingdom of the legendary Christian

Prester John in central Asia perpetuated the myths about him for many years.

It was at this stage of their journey that the Polos were met by messengers from Kublai Khan. The messengers had been instructed to welcome the Polos warmly and to escort them in comfort to the khan's favorite summer palace at Shangtu, about 180 miles northwest of Cambaluc and outside the Great Wall of China.

The last stage of their journey took some 40 days. The whole journey, from Hormuz, on the Persian Gulf, to the khan's summer palace had taken, according to Marco Polo's account, $3\frac{1}{2}$ years.

Below: an imaginary portrayal of the battle between Genghis Khan and Prester John. Despite Marco Polo's assurances, Prester John was a legendary character. *(Bodleian Library, Oxford. MS. Bodley 264, fol. 231v.)*

The Polos
in China

10

Kublai Khan was delighted with the arrival of the Venetian travelers at his court. At a public audience, he received the Polos and they honored him in the Mongol way by prostrating themselves several times at his feet. The khan was greatly pleased with the letters and presents from the pope, particularly with the bottle of holy oil from Jerusalem. Noticing the young Marco, the Khan inquired who he was. "Sire," said Nicolò, "He is my son and your liege man."

Marco Polo was at once enrolled among the khan's attendants of honor, and became a favorite and close friend. Marco was anxious to learn as much as he could about Mongol ways. Soon he was

Above: the Polos hand their letter
from the pope to the Great Khan at
the end of their 3½-year journey.
(*Bodleian Library, Oxford. MS. Bodley
264, fol. 220.*)

Left: the fabulous palace of the
Great Khan at Cambaluc. Marco Polo
said it was the largest ever seen,
with priceless treasures, and set in
beautiful parkland, full of game.

fluent in a number of Asian languages and quickly mastered the art
of writing four—possibly Baspa Mongolian, Arabic, Uighur and
Tibetan. He never, however, mastered Chinese script.

Influenced by Marco's charm and his obvious willingness to
learn, Kublai determined to try out the young Venetian as his
personal ambassador. He sent him on important and confidential
state business to a place some six months' journey from Cambaluc,
and, when Marco carried out this commission to the khan's satis-
faction, Kublai employed him as a full-time civil servant. He sent
him on secret missions to almost every part of the Mongol Empire.

From time to time Marco traveled on his own initiative, but always with the consent and sanction of the khan. During his 17 years in the khan's service, Marco covered great distances and saw more of the world than any European had ever done. As he says in the preface to *The Book of Marco Polo,* "to this day there has been no man, Christian or Pagan, Tartar or Italian, or of any race . . . who has explored so many of the various parts of the world and of its great wonders as this same . . . Marco Polo."

As far as we know, Marco's claim is perfectly valid. Certainly

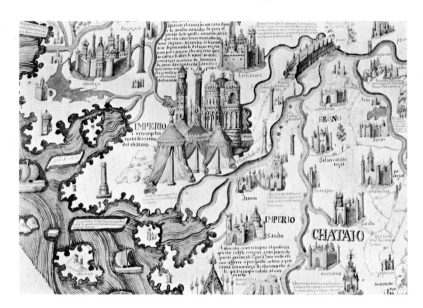

Left: part of a map of 1459, based on Marco Polo's description of Cambaluc. The artist has drawn a Western-style Renaissance city, with Kublai Khan's palace in the center.

some of the places he visited were not seen or written about again by Europeans until the middle of the 1800's. There must have been a number of Europeans—merchants, craftsmen, mercenaries, preachers—who made the long journey across the northern steppes and central deserts during Polo's time. Some of them must have penetrated to Mongolia and the borders of China. But none has left a record like Marco Polo's, and possibly no one saw as many wonders.

To Marco, reminiscing at the end of his long years in China, one of the most beautiful of all the sights he ever saw was the very first, the summer palace at Shangtu—the magical Xanadu of Coleridge's poem "Kubla Khan." When the Polos arrived in China, Kublai Khan was the most powerful man alive. The style in which he lived was far more lavish than that of any European monarch. The luxury and grandeur, which reached their peak during Kublai Khan's reign, were eventually to decline into a decadence and indulgence which proved disastrous for the Mongol empire. But in the 1260's and 1270's, the splendor of the Mongol court was at its height.

Shangtu was beautiful, but Cambaluc itself, the true capital, was amazing. After a summer spent in hunting and feasting at Shangtu, the whole court returned to Cambaluc around November. The first time Marco saw it, Cambaluc had recently been partly evacuated by Kublai because his astrologers had told him that an internal rebellion

was imminent. He had built an extension to the city at Tai-du, or Ta-du, northeast of the old town. The new city was built in a perfect square, six miles by six, and enclosed by a rampart 20 paces (approximately 50 feet) high. Polo's readers, who lived in cramped, twisting, medieval alleys, must have been startled to read of the city's spaciousness. It was full of fine mansions, with booths and shops edging each main street. Every block of buildings was surrounded by good, wide roads, and the whole interior of the city was laid out in squares like a chessboard "with such precision that no description can do justice to it."

Beyond the city walls were huge suburbs where there were palaces and hostels for the thousands of visiting merchants. To emphasize the size of this vast city, Polo adds that 1,000 cartloads of silk yarn were brought to the Cambaluc weavers every day.

Within the new city itself, stood the khan's palace—a city within a city. Inside the great fortress of the outer marble walls, stood the high-roofed main building, its interior "all gold and silver and decorated with pictures . . . the ceilings similarly adorned. . . ." The main hall was so vast that 6,000 men could be served there. "No man," Marco says, "could imagine any improvement in design and execution. The roof is all ablaze with scarlet and green and blue and yellow and all the colors . . . are so brilliantly varnished that

Above: the Great Khan out hunting. Marco Polo wrote about the royal hunting parties, which took place during the three months Kublai spent each year in Cambaluc. According to him, besides dogs, the khan hunted with leopards, lynxes, and even lions. *(Bodleian Library, Oxford. MS. Bodley 264, fol. 240v.)*

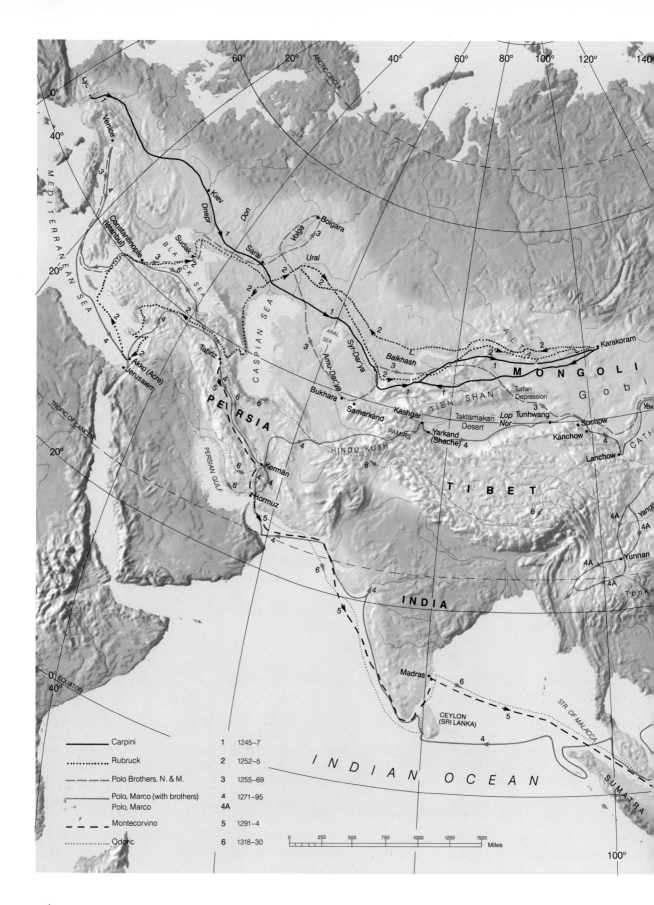

Left: Asia and eastern Europe, showing the routes of European travelers from Carpini to Odoric of Pordenone, from the mid-1200's to the mid-1300's.

Above: Marco Polo reported the Great Khan to be a charitable man. He is seen here handing alms to the poor. *(Bodleian Library, Oxford. MS. Bodley 264, fol. 244.)*

it glitters like crystal . . . the sparkle can be seen from far away." Around the park was a well-stocked game park with an artificial hill in it, planted with samples of the finest trees in the world. In 1275, Kublai was engaged in building another palace, equally vast and well equipped, for his son Chinkin.

Marco Polo often remarks on the khan's "stupendous munificence," and contemporary Asian writers also commend Kublai as brave, just, and generous. Living in great luxury himself, the khan was also aware of the problems of the poor people in his realm, and helped them "like a kind of father" as often as he could. At harvest time he sent inspectors throughout the land to inquire if any of his subjects had suffered a crop failure. For those who had, Kublai exempted them for that year from paying the statutory annual tax, and often gave them some of his own grain. In winter, he checked on the cattle of his subjects. If he heard that a man had lost cattle, he gave him some of his own. If he learned of an honest respectable family impoverished by misfortune or unfit for work through illness, the khan saw to it that the family was given money enough for a whole year's expenses. Officials appointed to superintend the khan's expenditure presided over the issuing to the needy of sums for subsistence. When a poor man could produce a certificate for the sum paid the previous year, they made provision for him to receive the same rate again. As a result, all the people held Kublai in such esteem that they revered him as a god.

Despite such bounty, the khan was still very rich. Marco's lists

Left: a garden near the Imperial Palace in present-day Peking. Many travelers mentioned the gardens of the Chinese capital, which were considered to be among the most beautiful in the world.

of his possessions are almost endless: 12,000 costly robes of cloth of gold given by the khan to his leading knights; 156,000 robes studded with gems and pearls for the same knights for the 13 great feasts of the year; 100,000 white horses; 100,000 personal servants; 5,000 elephants, each bearing 2 giant chests of precious gems, gold plate, and rich apparel; camels beyond number; 10,000 falconers; tents lined with thousands of sable furs, each fur costing over $5,000 by today's prices . . . and so on, and so on.

To many of Marco Polo's European readers these lists seemed

Above: the Chinese not only invented paper, but were the first nation to use paper currency. Marco thought this ability to ''make'' money caused the khan's wealth, not realizing that he could only issue money up to the value of stocks of gold and silver. Here the khan is seen supervising the distribution of paper money.

unbelievable. People were unable to grasp how vast was the empire Kublai governed and from which he took tribute. Even Marco, who eventually traveled the length and most of the breadth of Kublai Khan's domain, misunderstood the source of most of his wealth. Marco thought the secret lay in the emperor's ability to print paper money—something then unknown anywhere in the world outside Asia. Marco also thought that Kublai had invented paper money, not knowing it had been common in China since at least the 800's and that Friar William of Rubruck had mentioned its existence in the 1250's. Marco did not realize that the gold and silver which merchants deposited against the issue of paper money was the real strength behind it. The Great Khan, however, printed far more money than could be backed by his gold and silver. This resulted in great inflation and a devaluation of the currency in 1287.

One of Marco's first official missions was a visit of inspection to the province of Yunnan, in southern China, and beyond. On this, and on trips he made in eastern China, Marco was given a chance to exercise his powers of observation and his interest in alien customs and beliefs. In the usual manner, he lists all the towns, cities, villages, and rivers he saw—their size, trade, manufacture, wealth, and importance to the khan. He also describes the long journeys between towns through remote rural areas or through mountain districts where the road was often little more than a plank walk shored up with timbers along precipitous bluffs.

In "Tibet," probably not the Tibet we know today but the western edges of Szechwan and Yunnan, Marco saw how travelers frightened off marauding lions and bears by burning giant canes. The explosions from these freshly cut and still sap-filled canes echoed for miles around and terrified anyone who was not used to them.

In some sections, Polo's account reads like a modern anthropological survey. He has a fair claim indeed to be called the father of modern anthropology (the study of man). For instance, he noted one tribe with a very strange birth custom. On the birth of a baby the husband took the child and went to rest in bed while the woman went straight back to her household work. This practice is called *couvade*. Anthropologists have since found it in places as far apart as Africa and the Amazon forests.

Another custom noted by Polo among the tribes in remote places and by later observers among other primitive peoples, was their habit of eating any person of rank or quality—anyone with a "good shadow"—who happened to stay the night. This was not done in order to rob the visitor, it was rather because they believed "his 'good shadow' and the good grace with which he was blessed and his intelligence and soul would remain in the house." According to Marco, this belief caused many deaths before the Mongol conquest, but the practice had later been forbidden by the khan.

The men of one tribe had gold-capped teeth. Another tribe used cowrie shells for money. Here they prevented their horses from swishing their tails by removing two or three of the tail bones.

Right: the custom of *couvade*, in which a wife got up immediately after giving birth, while her husband took to his bed with the baby, was reported by Marco Polo to occur in Burma. It still takes place today among some primitive communities. *(Bodleian Library, Oxford. MS. Bodley 264, fol. 249v.)*

Above: the gold and silver towers which Marco Polo reported seeing when he visited the Burmese city of Mien. *(Bodleian Library, Oxford. MS. Bodley 264, fol. 251v.)*

There they rode with their stirrups long "as the Latins do." Every oddity caught Marco's attentive eye.

In a Burmese city, Marco saw one of the wonders of Southeast Asia—a local king's tomb with two towers, one of gold, one of silver. Both towers were fully 10 paces (25 feet) high and circular, and were set with gilded bells which tinkled every time the wind blew. Kublai refused to have these unique towers dismantled and taken to Cambaluc because Mongols would never disturb the property of the dead.

On his return from Burma, Polo seems to have made a detour to the east. He journeyed through the provinces of Caugigu and Anin, which were situated near the present northern borders of Laos and Vietnam. Some time later, Marco made a similar journey down through eastern China. For a number of years he was Kublai's personal representative in the city of Yang-chou near the Yangtze River. He probably covered the ground between Cambaluc and Yang-chou many times. The *Book* declares that Marco Polo was governor of Yang-chou but there is no evidence to support the claim. Polo may also have made the rest of the journey south, down as far as Amoy, Mandarin Hsia-men, on the mainland opposite Taiwan, during his years of service with the khan. He certainly did so when he left China toward the close of the century.

While Marco was traveling, the elder Polos stayed in or near the court of the khan. Little is known of their activities, but they were engaged in some kind of commerce, and most profitably. Like Marco, they became extremely rich.

Despite their many privileges as Kublai's friends, the Polos longed to see Venice again. The yearning grew stronger and stronger

Right: a painting of Marco Polo dressed in Mongolian-style clothes. Being young, he was able to travel widely, while his father and uncle stayed nearer to the khan's court.

Above: this illumination from a copy of Marco Polo's *Book* shows the weird creatures he thought lived in India. *(Bodleian Library, Oxford. MS. Bodley 264, fol. 260.)*

Right: Arghun, ruler of Persia, in his garden. The Polos finally left Kublai Khan's court in the retinue of Arghun's Mongolian bride, whom they escorted to Persia.

as the years passed. Time and again they asked the khan to let them go home, but Kublai was fond of them, and they had become useful to him. Nothing would persuade him to let them go. The Polos were concerned by the fact that Kublai was now in his 70's and could not be expected to live much longer. There was no guarantee that his successor, or the regent, would grant the Polos the same favors and privileges. Like all courts, the one at Cambaluc was full of intrigue and broken bargains, and the Polos had acquired enemies as well as friends in their years in China.

Then chance gave them the perfect excuse for returning home. Queen Bulagan, wife of the Persian khan Arghun, died in 1286. She had stipulated in her will that her successor should come from her own tribe in Mongolia. So Arghun sent envoys overland, probably following the route the Polos had taken nearly 15 years earlier, to ask for a young, unmarried noblewoman of Bulagan's lineage for his next wife. Kublai granted his request and envoys set out on the return journey with the princess.

Eight months later they were back again in Cambaluc. Their route had been blocked by an outbreak of intertribal wars like those common among the Mongols before the days of Genghis Khan.

Marco Polo returned in about 1290 from an official mission to India, of which he gives no details except to say that part of the voyage had been by ship. He reported that the sea passage to India was open and safe. Hearing this, the envoys begged Kublai to let

the Polos, known to be experienced sea travelers, escort them along the sea route to Persia. Kublai reluctantly agreed. He gave the Polos passports stamped on gold, letters and gifts for the pope and princes of Christendom, and presents for themselves. He fitted out a fleet of 14 ships, 5 of them large enough to need crews of 260 men. All the vessels were divided into watertight sections. This meant that if the ship were holed, the flooding could be confined to that section of the hull.

With mingled joy and sorrow, the four old friends parted for the last time in 1292—Kublai, then 76, Marco still only 38, and Nicolò and Maffeo now elderly men. The Polos set out on the familiar road southwest from Cambaluc, the great highway along which Marco had begun most of his travels in the khan's service. A large section of the route ran down the Grand Canal, the giant man-made river that is still one of China's most important waterways. Marco Polo

Left: a group of merchants returning two girls to their fathers and
offering them jewels. According to
Marco Polo, it was an accepted custom in some parts of China for girls
to live with men before being married.

thought that Kublai had built this canal and the broad, stone-paved
avenues that flanked it. In fact, it had been created by the Chinese
much earlier—as long ago as A.D. 605–610, and certain sections are
thought to date from the 300's B.C. They had joined up existing rivers
and lakes and cut new channels. Kublai had only restored the canal
and extended it to the outskirts of Cambaluc.

Marco's unflagging eye and memory were as busy as ever throughout the journey home. At Ts'ang-chou, pure, white, fine-grained salt
was produced and he describes the method. The province around
T'sin-nan-fu produced "silk past all reckoning" and the city itself
had "many delightful gardens full of excellent fruit."

Marco the anthropologist adds notes on the appearance and
demeanor of the young ladies of Cathay, whose modesty and de-
corum he much admired. He praises, too, their custom of never
speaking to an older person unless first spoken to. He fills several

more pages with observations of marriage customs, beliefs, oracles, and the like.

Near Ts'ang-chou in central China, the Polos saw one of the engineering wonders of the Grand Canal. Chinese engineers with great skill had partially diverted the Wen River so that some of its waters flowed north. As a result, in this region the canal was comprised of two branches of the same waterway. One flowed north toward the capital, Cambaluc, and the other flowed southward toward the fertile grain-growing regions of southeastern China. Boats

Right: Chinese women pulling a barge along the Grand Canal, near Suchow. This vital waterway was constructed in the 600's and was later restored and extended by Kublai Khan.

were able to free float in either direction on the same waterway.

Polo tells us that the Yellow River then ran between Haui-an and Ching-chiang—the only clue he gives us to its course at that date. In 1852, as many times earlier, the river burst its banks and changed course to run along a more northerly channel than in the 1200's. Polo says that the Yellow River was more than a mile wide and the cities on its banks held 15,000 of the khan's military ships, each kept ready with a crew of 20 to carry up to 15 troopers, their mounts and provisions. It was such an armada that the khan sent on an

ill-fated expedition to conquer Japan in 1281, when the army was routed by the Japanese and the khan's fleet destroyed by a typhoon. Polo gives the full history of the ill-fated and mismanaged campaign, including the terrible punishment handed out to the two commanders. One was beheaded, the other marooned on an island with his hands bound in freshly flayed buffalo hide, tightly sewn. As it dried, it tightened further and he died either of gangrene or starvation.

Curiously enough, Polo tells us next to nothing of Yang-chou, the city he says he governed. But he gives a fascinating picture of the Yangtze River at Iching Hein, farther south:

". . . in the amount of shipping it carries and the total volume of traffic it exceeds all the rivers of the Christians put together and their seas into the bargain. I give you my word that I have seen in this city [Iching Hein] fully 15,000 ships at once, all afloat in this river . . . I assure you that the river flows through more than 16 provinces, and there are on its banks more than 200 cities, all having more ships than this . . . fully 200,000 craft pass upstream every year and a like number return." Marco also explains how the ships were hauled upstream by teams of horses hitched to the bows by long towropes.

The highlight of the Chinese part of this journey was a visit to the mighty city of Hangchow. The Polos had arrived in China shortly before Kublai extended his rule to the whole country. For the Chinese, his was the last of a whole series of nomad conquests extending over the centuries. Kublai broke the back of the Sung dynasty, the guardian of China's ancient civilization. For though Kublai was a wise and far-seeing ruler, the Chinese under him were

Left: this detail from a map of 1459, shows the Chinese city of Zaitun near Amoy. Zaitun (now Ch'üan-chou) was the port from which the Polos embarked on their return journey.

a conquered people and were culturally stifled. This cultural decline was just beginning in Marco's time and would not be reversed until the restoration of a native Chinese dynasty, the Mings, in the 1300's. For this reason alone, his picture of Hangchow, one of China's foremost cities, gives a unique and priceless insight into that vanished greatness.

Hangchow was about 100 miles in circumference and housed 1,600,000 families. Marco says that there were 12,000 bridges in Hangchow, some so high-arched that tall-masted ships could navigate beneath them. But they were also gently pitched so that wheeled traffic could easily pass over them. All streets were paved in stone and the main roads had storm drainage.

There were 10 main squares, each holding thrice-weekly markets visited by up to 50,000 people in search of everything from rare pearls to such staple foods as meat, fish, game, fruit, and herbs.

Marco says five tons of pepper were sold there daily. There were hundreds of smaller local markets, too.

The city's industry was managed by a dozen craft guilds each with about 12,000 workshops employing between 12 and 40 craftsmen. For the very wealthy workshop owners and their richly dressed wives and children, the pleasures of life centered on the sumptuous pavilions around the islands of the city lake. These were fully furnished for parties and banquets. Over 100 banquets could be held there simultaneously. On the lake and through the canals plied innumerable pleasure boats with ornate and comfortable cabins.

The city was a leading center of education, art, and culture, with more library books than any other Chinese city. But the shadow of the Great Khan was everywhere. Each of the bridges housed at least five guards to check insurrection. Every hotelkeeper was obliged to record the names of each visitor, where he came from, and where he was bound. "A useful piece of knowledge," Marco says, "to prudent statesmen."

Marco, who was present at many reckonings, puts the total tax

Below: Indian ships, described in some detail by Marco Polo. *(Bodleian Library, Oxford. MS. Bodley 264, fol. 259v.)*

revenue from Hangchow at over 3,250,000 ounces of gold, of which the salt duty alone contributed almost 1,000,000.

From Hangchow the Polos continued south to Zaitun, in medieval times the great port of southern China near Amoy. Details of this stage of the journey are skimpy and it is impossible to plot their route with certainty.

The Book of Marco Polo describes the long voyage home by sea. The Venetians stopped in Indochina, Ceylon (Sri Lanka), India and Persia, but the visits were short and Marco's descriptions are not as detailed as those of Cambaluc and Hangchow. Marco's geography is generally accurate. So, too, is most of the information he gives on the trade and produce of each country. He has a lot to say, for instance, of the gems mined in Ceylon and of the pearl-diving industry in the nearby Indian waters. But the highlight of the homeward section is Marco's penetrating and sympathetic observation of Indian religions. He gives a fairly accurate paraphrase of the life story of the Indian who became the Buddha and acquired a deep respect for his saintly lifestyle. He wrote unsympathetically, however, of the Hindus and their gods and yogis.

The wealth of India impressed Marco greatly and he described it all in glowing terms. This account of the vast subcontinent proved of great interest in Europe, and by 1315, Genoese merchants had established trading stations in India.

But it is Marco's love of—and obvious nostalgia for—China that is the lasting impression in the reader's mind at the end of *The Book of Marco Polo*. When he left, Marco knew that he would probably never return to the lands of the Great Khan. Even before he and his father and uncle got back to Venice Kublai had died, leaving behind a great Mongol empire, which, however, was destined to decay rapidly following his death.

In 1298, Polo was captured by the Genoese in the course of a war against Venice and thrown into the same jail as the writer Rusticello. To while away the days, he told of his adventures in far-off Cathay with such a wealth of detail that those who started listening in disbelief soon knew he was telling the truth. His cellmate Rusticello, seeing his great chance, persuaded Polo to collaborate in setting down the whole story. Polo agreed and sent to Venice for his notes and diaries. Later published as *The Book of Marco Polo*, Marco's story was for a long time disbelieved as being too fantastic to be true. Nevertheless, it had a resounding popular success. And, more than 150 years after it had been written, it provided inspiration for the great explorers of the 1400's.

In 1299, Venice and Genoa signed a truce and all prisoners of war were freed. Marco Polo went back to Venice and, after the death of his father and uncles, started trading as his forefathers had always done. He settled down, married, had a family, and never traveled again. According to legend, when he was dying, in 1324, friends asked Marco whether he would not correct the exaggerations of his story. He answered, "I did not write half of what I saw."

Right: the courtyard and gateway, now part of a more recent building, are all that remain today of Marco Polo's house in Venice. It was called Court of the Million because he was often called "Marco the Million" as he frequently used the term "million" to describe the wealth of the Orient.

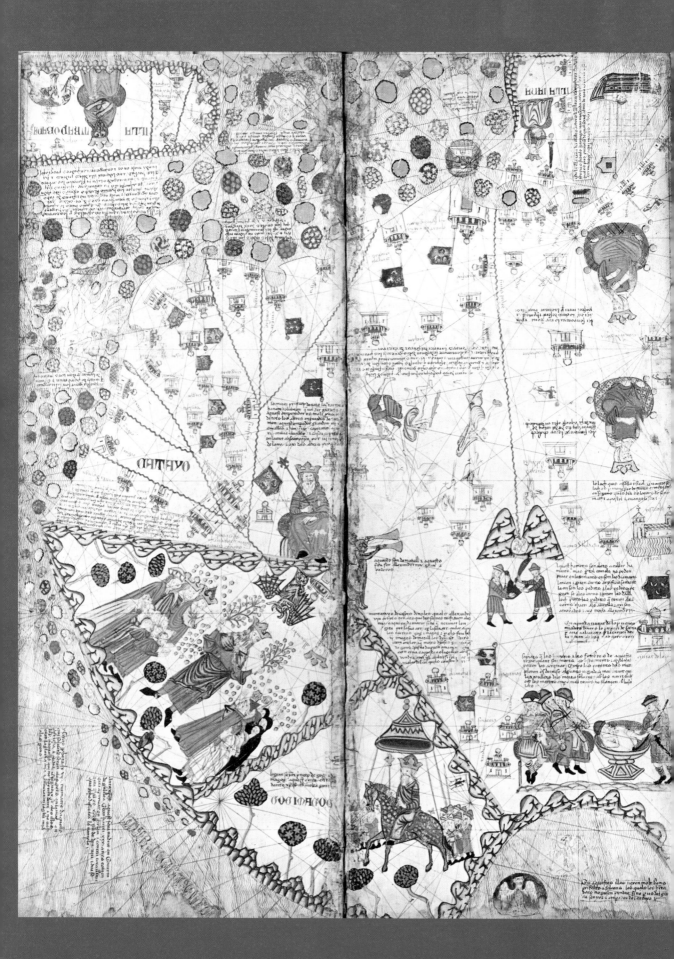

Missionaries to Cambaluc

11

Left: a detail from the famous Catalan map of the world, prepared in 1375 for the king of France. It shows a striking advance on other medieval maps, which were largely guesswork. Much of its information was based on *portolan*, or seamen's, charts—the first maps to use proper compass references. This decorative detail of part of the Chinese coastline and interior owed a good deal to the firsthand reports of Marco Polo and subsequent travelers.

Above: Pope Nicholas IV, like his predecessor Innocent IV, had hopes of converting the eastern khans to Christianity. In 1291, he sent out the missionary John of Montecorvino to try to achieve this aim.

For about 50 years after the Polos' return to Venice, the trade routes through Asia to Cathay remained open and safe, and trade with the Far East prospered. China and the East were visited by so many merchants that, in 1340, one merchant called Pegolotti set down his favorite route for the use of other travelers. A welcome was extended to religious travelers as well. The ambassadors of the four main religions, Buddhism, Christianity, Confucianism, and Islam, were entertained and given a hearing in the khan's capital at Cambaluc. The khan and his leading citizens entertained representatives of all religions at court, and attended ceremonies in each of the religious centers established by the foreigners in Cambaluc. Possibly the Mongol open-mindedness was the result of a desire to be on the right side, religiously speaking, by being on all sides. They may have thought that by listening to the prayers of holy men of all religions they were ensuring themselves some sort of passport to a happy afterlife. Whatever the reason, there was unprecedented and unique liberal-mindedness and freedom of speech and thought in China during the period of Mongol occupation.

Christian missionaries took the road east by land and by sea. They were determined to seize the chance of converting the Mongols which had been lost by the two Dominican friars who had deserted the Polos at Layas. One of the most notable of the missionaries was a Franciscan friar called John of Montecorvino. Montecorvino was born in a village in southern Italy in 1247. As a young man, he took part in missions to Armenia and Persia, and spent a period of about 14 years traveling in the Middle East. Afterward, he returned to Europe and reported to Pope Nicholas IV his high hopes of being able to convert the Khan of Persia, Arghun. If Arghun were converted to the Catholic faith, all of his subjects would follow suit. Pope Nicholas was highly pleased by this news, and decided to send Montecorvino back to Asia carrying letters to all patriarchs and princes of the East, including Kublai Khan and Kaidu, the khan of the house of Ogotai in central Asia, who was Kublai's bitterest enemy.

In 1291, as the Polos were at last about to leave China, John of Montecorvino left from Tabriz in Persia on the first stage of his journey, in the company of a rich and friendly Italian merchant named Pietro of Lucolongo. Pietro was familiar with trade routes in the Middle East and central Asia, and was, therefore, a valuable

Above: John of Montecorvino succeeded in founding Catholic communities in both India and China, although reports that he had baptized the Great Khan himself were not verified. In 1307, the pope made him Archbishop of Cambaluc and Patriarch of the Orient.

companion. They made their way to Hormuz and sailed from there to southern India.

The party spent a period of about a year in India, their stay occasioned by the outbreak of a violent war between Kublai and Kaidu. During his time there, Montecorvino visited the sacred place called Saint Thomas' Shrine, near Madras, where the body of "Doubting Thomas" was buried. He also baptized, as he claims in a later report to the pope, about 400 persons. In 1294, Kublai died and was succeeded by his grandson Timur Oljaitu. Shortly afterward, Montecorvino reached China.

In the same letter to the pope, dated 1305, Montecorvino tells of the near 13 years he had spent working diligently in Cathay, helped occasionally by the merchant Pietro and joined "only recently" by a friar, Arnold of Cologne. Timur appeared sympathetic to the Christian's endeavors, but gave him little practical help. Montecorvino's main success in those first dozen years seems to have been his conversion of a follower of the Nestorian sect, a nobleman called George "of the family of Prester John."

George was the ruler of the Kereyids of eastern Mongolia. George supplied the money for the building of a beautiful Catholic church 20 days' journey from Cambaluc, possibly in Tenduc. Unfortunately for Montecorvino, and for the growth of Chinese Christianity, George soon died. Montecorvino had to report to the pope with much regret that the Kereyids had reverted to the Nestorian version of the faith.

Montecorvino had some other successes in his long hard-working years away from home. He worked diligently in the capital and succeeded in establishing an active center of Mongol Catholicism. Six years before writing his letter, he had been given permission and assistance by Timur Khan to build a church in Cambaluc. The priest had assembled the rudiments of a choir and had "gradually brought [into the faith] 150 boys, the children of pagan parents . . . 11 of the boys already know the service and form a choir. His majesty the emperor delights to hear them chanting."

The pope was so impressed by Montecorvino's optimistic report of conditions in China that he officially appointed Montecorvino Archbishop of Cambaluc and sent seven Franciscans out to China to help him. Three of them died on the way, unable to withstand their first experience of the Indian climate. One turned back while

Right: a form of Christianity—the Nestorian church—which originated in the Middle East, had made converts in central Asia, and even reached Mongolia and China, some centuries before the Catholic missions arrived. Its clergy became increasingly Oriental in outlook, and the religion soon lost its impetus. The woman depicted in this Nestorian religious painting has typically Chinese features.

the others reached China where they worked under the leadership of Montecorvino. They served in succession as bishops of Zaitun.

For more than 20 years, the Christian mission in China flourished under Archbishop John. After he died, having been the first and last effective Archbishop of Cambaluc, the mission lost much of its vigor. A French friar called Nicholas was appointed as Montecorvino's successor, and set out with a party of 20 friars and 6 laymen. Nothing is known of their fate, but they did not reach the court of Cathay. The movement struggled on for 40 years, ever weakening, before dying out almost completely. The last medieval Catholic bishop in China was martyred in 1362, and in 1369, the Christians were expelled from Cambaluc, not to return until the French missionaries of the early 1600's.

An account of the missionary activities in China toward the end of John of Montecorvino's life is given in the contemporary *Journal of Friar Odoric*. Odoric of Pordenone, in Italy, was a Franciscan friar. As a young man he was renowned among the members of his order for his asceticism. He always went barefoot, and always wore either haircloth or ironmail shirts as a denial of luxury and comfort. He lived mainly on a diet of water and a very little bread.

Around 1318, Friar Odoric was sent to the East as part of an extension of the Catholic missionary movement into Asia. From then on he became addicted to travel. First he visited India, where he arrived in 1321.

As Montecorvino had done, Odoric visited Saint Thomas' Shrine near Madras. Taking with him the bones of martyrs as sacred relics, Odoric sailed to the East Indies. After landing at Sumatra and Java, he sailed to Borneo, where he recorded that the islanders used deadly blowpipes, the first mention of these in European writing. Then he returned to Cambaluc by way of southern China.

Odoric was the first traveler after Marco Polo to leave a full written account of all the places he had visited and seen. He gives details of the customs and peoples he observed in many countries. He also vividly describes the scenery and buildings in places he passed through.

Like Marco Polo, Odoric describes Cambaluc as a beautiful, enviable place, superior to even a major city in Europe in its luxury and attractiveness. He describes its beautiful buildings and spacious roads, and gives a detailed account of the khan's palace and court, and of the lavish ceremonies which took place there. The Great Khan celebrated four major feast days in the year. On these occasions all the khan's barons, his musicians, his stage-players and "everyone of his kindred" were invited to eat at the palace. Friar Odoric was not favorably impressed by some of the ceremonies which took place on those occasions. Often he disapproved of what seemed to him a foolish exercise of the khan's absolute rule over his people. He writes of one such occasion: "When the time is come . . . a certain crier calls out with a loud voice saying 'Bow yourselves before your emperor.' With that all the barons fall flat upon the earth. Then

Right: the court of Tamerlane, a descendant of Genghis Khan. In its riches and splendor, the court of Tamerlane equaled that of the earlier Mongol emperors, and this picture gives a good idea of the magnificence of that court.

萬曆己未出地崇禎戊寅摹勒

泉郡南邑西山古石聖架碑式

Above: John of Montecorvino's success in China was short-lived. Some forty years after his death, Peking expelled its Christian community. Soon, little remained to show that it had ever existed, apart from sober reminders such as this drawing of a missionary's last resting place.

اگر فیروزی آثار که بنگا مشی در عقب گریخیگان رفته بوند سلطان محمود خان

یدرم یا بزید بر سیده و او را و تیکه کرده و دست بسته بدرگاه عالم پناه آورد

Right: Friar Odoric leaving on his
travels to Asia. His journey took
him overland to Hormuz, by sea to India, and then on to China. Odoric's
account of his three-year stay in
China, during which he visited Cambaluc and Hangchow, was the most in-
formative after that of Marco Polo.

he cries 'Arise all.' And immediately they all arise. Likewise . . . he
cries 'Put your fingers in your ears.' And again . . . 'Pluck them
out'. . . . At the third point he calls: 'Bolt this meal'. . . . And when
the musicians' hour is come, then the philosophers say 'Solemnize
a feast unto your Lord.' With that all sound their instruments. . . .
And immediately another cries 'Peace, peace,' and they all cease."

But, in general, Odoric appreciated the treatment he himself
received from the khan. "I, Friar Odoric, was present in person at
[the khan's] palace. For we minor friars have a place of abode appointed
out for us in the emperor's court and are enjoined to go and bestow
our blessing upon him."

At the time of Odoric's visit there were 400 heathen and eight
Christian physicians, and one Moslem in permanent residence in
the court. They were all supplied by the khan with everything

that they required in the way of food and clothing.

Like Marco Polo before him, Odoric tells of the marvelous road and communications system that prevailed right across the empire. "The emperor so that travelers may have all things necessary throughout his whole empire has caused certain inns to be provided upon the highways where all things pertaining to victuals are in a continual readiness. And when any news happens in any part of his empire, if he chance to be far absent from that part his messengers upon horses or dromedaries ride post to him, and when they and their beasts are weary, they blow their horn, and at the noise of it the next inn likewise provides a horse and a man who takes the letter of him that is weary, and runs to another inn. And so by many inns, and many posts, the report which ordinarily could scarcely come in 30 days, is in one natural day brought to the emperor. Therefore no

Above: a fragment from a manuscript of 1444 describing Odoric's journey to the lands of the infidel (Mongols). Odoric traveled in the Middle East before setting out for China.

Left: a city gate in Peking. The Mongols ruled in Cambaluc until 1368, when the Chinese rebelled and drove them out, together with the last khan, Toghon-Timur. The Chinese then established the Ming dynasty and renamed the city Peiping (later Peking).

happening of any moment can be done in his empire but straightway he has intelligence thereof."

After three years in Cathay, Odoric set off overland across Asia, through Tibet and Persia, and home to Italy. On this journey, too, he made notes on several lands through which he passed including Tibet. Odoric was probably the first European to leave a record of having visited Lhasa, the Tibetan holy city.

A letter to Pope Benedict in Avignon, in 1338, from the Great Khan led to the last important medieval mission to China. The Khan asked for the pope's benediction, and included in his letter a commendation of the Christian Alans, inhabitants of the far western part of his empire.

He asked for horses and other souvenirs of the West—"land of the sunset." In answer to his request the pope sent out an embassy headed by a man called John Marignolli. The mission left Avignon (where the papal court had been held since 1309) in 1338, and traveled by land to Cambaluc, which was reached in 1342. The ambassadors enjoyed royal hospitality for a period of about four years, and then returned to Europe by the sea route Marco Polo had taken. Very little is known about the Marignolli mission, but it is recorded that the Christians presented the Mongol emperor with a war horse $11\frac{1}{2}$ feet long and 6 feet 8 inches high. More Chinese writings survive about the horse, which was a great wonder to them,

Above: Odoric met the people as well as the nobility during his travels. In Mongolia, local trade depended much on itinerant peddlers. One is seen here with his family.

Left: all the Christian missionaries were impressed by the high level of Chinese culture. Literary gatherings, as shown in this painting, with women serving tea, must have been common among the educated classes.

than about the priests who presented it, in whom they showed little interest. With the end of this mission, all evangelizing expeditions from Europe to China ceased until the early 1600's.

After Kublai Khan's death, the Mongols declined in power and prestige. Their leaders dedicated themselves more and more to personal luxury and comfort rather than to the development and care of the existing empire, and were so weakened that, in 1368, a Chinese leader came to power. Two years later, the Mongols were driven out of China and back to their homeland, and the gates to the Far East closed behind them.

European travelers had achieved a great deal during the 10 centuries between 400 and 1400. Irish missionaries had ventured out into the Atlantic Ocean. The Vikings had sailed far to the west to Iceland, Greenland, and the northeast shores of the American continent. The Polos and a handful of dedicated priests and friars had traveled amazing distances overland across Asia, to trade with the Mongols and Chinese, and convert them to Christianity. But none of these achievements had any real lasting value. The Viking attempt to settle on the coast of Greenland was a failure. During the 1400's, disease, a worsening of the harsh climate, or Eskimo attacks wiped out all the little colonies. The settlements established in Vinland by Karlsefni and Freydis had been shortlived. Only Iceland remained, a colony first of the Norwegian and then of the Danish kings, until it became an independent republic in 1944.

The European travelers in the Far East also achieved little in the long term. Europeans in the 1400's knew less about China and

Below: education in Mongol China was reserved for the privileged minority of town dwellers. The huge rural population was poor and illiterate, leading a rugged existence, as depicted in this contemporary drawing.

Cy commence le chemin de la pelerginacion et du
voyage que fist vn bon homme de lordre des freres
meneurs nomme frere odric de fric uili ne de vne
terre que on appelle port de vauisse qui par le comās
du pape ala oultre mer pour preschier sur mesare
ans la foy de dieu. Et sont en ce liure contenu los
merueilles que li dis freres vit presentment, et aul
sy de pluseurs autres lesquelles il oy compter en ces
parties sus dittes de gens dignes de foy. Mais celles quil oy racompter et
quil ne vit point. ne racompte il point pour verite fors pour oir dire. et le co
ne en son langaige quant a ce vient. Et fu ce liure fait en latin par ce frere de
uant nomme en lan de grace mil. CCC. xxx. puis le .xiij. iour de ianuier

Left: an illumination from *Les Livres Merveilles,* showing Friar Odoric (kneeling left) being blessed before setting out on his long journey to the East. Much of our information about this otherwise confused period of history comes from manuscripts painstakingly handwritten and occasionally beautifully illuminated, and preserved today in the world's museums.

had less contact with its people than they had in the 1200's. There were two main reasons for this. In 1370, the Chinese drove out the Mongols from China, back to the windswept plains of central Asia from which they had originally come. The collapse of the Mongol Empire, with its superb system of roads and way stations across Asia, and the readiness of its rulers to receive traders and Christian missionaries from Europe, was a disaster for East-West relations. All contact between China and the West came to an end. Never again would China be as open to Western travelers, trade, and ideas as it

Above: this ancient bridge near Peking is named after Marco Polo, the traveler who successfully forged a link between East and West 700 years ago. Peking today consists of two cities. The Inner City in the north lies more or less on the site of the old Mongol capital of Cambaluc.

had been under the khans. Historians have even suggested that people in the West in the 1200's knew more about China than we do today, although communication in the 1970's and 80's was improved.

There was another serious obstacle to European contact and trade with the Far East after the mid-1300's. In 1345, an army of Ottoman Turks—at the time unequaled in military skill and organization—crossed the narrow straits, now called the Dardanelles, that separate Europe and Asia, and attacked the southeast corner of Christendom. In May, 1453, after just over a hundred years of intermittent warfare against the armies of Christian Europe, Sultan Mohammed led a triumphant army into the city of Constantinople. For three days the Turkish soldiers plundered, terrorized, and destroyed the city, which for centuries had been the capital of eastern Christianity. The fall of Constantinople and the rise of an aggressive Islamic empire in the eastern Mediterranean meant that the main gateway of the overland route to China and the Far East was closed. Turkish and Arab middlemen controlled the Far Eastern trade routes, and the European end of the trade was handled almost solely by the Italian city-states of Venice and Genoa. From now on, Europeans had to look for new routes to the fabulous wealth of the Orient.

Above: by the 1400's, thanks to the reports of missionaries and merchants, mapmakers were able to fill in important features, previously missing, on their atlases. In Venice, the monk Fra Mauro completed his world map in 1459. Africa and Asia, though still inaccurate in many respects, are drawn with a wealth of detail. Like most maps of the middle ages, it shows the world as a flat disk surrounded by sea, with south at the top and north at the bottom.

But in spite of this abrupt shutting out of European travelers from Asia and the Far East, the achievements of Marco Polo and the missionaries were not entirely wasted. A small Christian community survived in China until the next wave of European missionaries arrived by sea in the 1600's. And it seems almost certain that Christopher Columbus was inspired by *The Book of Marco Polo* to attempt to reach the Orient by sailing the other way around the world—to the west. So it was that an account of a Venetian merchant about the East led Columbus to rediscover, quite by accident, the continent in the West that the Vikings had found, colonized and subsequently abandoned.

The Explorers

King Louis IX (Saint Louis) setting out on the first of his two Crusades.

ARNASON, INGÓLFUR
800's   Norway
870: Sailed to Iceland with foster
brother Leif Hrodmarsson. Explored
Alptafjord, but did not settle there.
874–877: Returned to Iceland.
Wintered at Ingolfshofdi, south of
Vatnajökull. Later founded first
permanent community in Iceland in
area between Olfusa River and
Hjalfjord, north of Reykjavik.

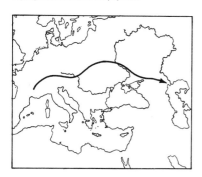

ASCELIN
dates unknown   France
1247–1248: Sent by Pope Innocent IV
on a mission to the Great Khan.
Thought to have retraced Carpini's
route as far as Mongol camp west of
Caspian Sea. Returned to Lyon with
letter from Mongol khan.

BRENDAN, SAINT
484–577   Ireland
Thought to have visited the Faeroes,
the Shetlands, and other Atlantic islands
on missionary voyages. Known to have
traveled from Ireland to Scotland,

Wales, and possibly Brittany.
See map on page 53

CARPINI, GIOVANNI DE PIANO
1182–1252   Italy
1245–1247: Sent by Pope Innocent IV
on mission to the Great Khan. Traveled
across Asia passing rivers Dnepr, Don,
Volga, and Ural, across the land north of
the Caspian Sea, then southeastward
through Syr-Darya Valley and along
the Tien Shan Mountains to khan's
summer court at Syra Orda in Mongolia.
See map on page 126

ERIC THE RED
900's   Norway
982: Sailed west from Iceland. Spent
three years exploring the west coast
of Greenland. Returned to the Icelandic
community.
985: Sailed back to found colony
centred at his homestead Brattahlid
near present-day Julianehåb. Colony
later called the Eastern Settlement.
See map on page 53

ERICSON, LEIF
900's–1000's   Iceland
1000(?): Sailed westward from
Herjulfsness in Greenland. Reached the
coasts of Helluland (possibly Baffin
Island), and Markland (possibly
Newfoundland or Labrador). Went
ashore southwest of Markland and
wintered in Vinland (thought to be the
mainland coast of North America
somewhere between Newfoundland
and Long Island).

ERICSON, THORWALD
900's–1000's   Iceland or Greenland
About 1002: Set out for Vinland.
Camped at Leifsbudir, in Vinland, then
sailed to Kjalarnes and Krossanes.
Killed by Skraelings (Indians).
See map on page 53

FREYDIS
900's–1000's   Iceland
1006(?): Initiated last Norse attempt
to settle in Vinland. Sailed to Leifsbudir.
A quarrel broke out among the settlers,
and Freydis organized the murder of
her enemies. Returned to Greenland.
See map top of next column

HERJULFSSON, BJARNI
900's   Iceland
986: Set out from Iceland for
Greenland, but driven off course.
Sighted the coast of an unknown
land thought to have been
North America.
See map on page 53

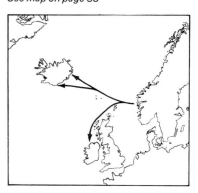

HRODMARSSON, LEIF
(HJÖRLEIF)
800's   Norway
870: Sailed to Iceland with foster
brother Ingólfur Arnason. Explored
Alptafjord area.
874–877: Returned to Iceland. Settled
at Mýrdalssandr on site
known as Hjörleifshofdi.
Murdered by Irish slaves.

KARLSEFNI, THORFINN
900's–1000's   Iceland
1005–1006(?): Sailed from Iceland to
Greenland, then to Vinland in an attempt
to start settlement there. Returned to
Greenland after battles with Skraelings

(local American Indians).
See map on page 53

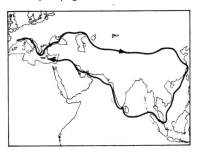

MARIGNOLLI, JOHN
dates unknown   Italy
1338: Left Avignon in France on last
important religious mission to China.
1342: Reached Cambaluc and began
four-year stay there.
1353: Reached Avignon
after following the sea route home
taken by the Polos.

MONTECORVINO, JOHN OF
1247–1328   Italy
1291: Set out on religious mission to
the court of the khan. Left Tabriz in
Persia, journeyed by sea to southern
India, spending a year there.
1294: Reached China.
1299: Established Roman Catholic
church in Cambaluc.
1307: Appointed Archbishop of
Cambaluc by Pope Nicholas IV.
See map on page 126

NADDOD
800's   Norway
860–870(?): An early Viking to reach

Iceland. Driven off course, landed at
Reydarfjord in the Austfirthir.

ODORIC OF PORDENONE
1274(?)–1331   Italy
About 1318: Sent to the East in
extension of Christian missions into
Asia.
1322: Reached China, having visited
Madras, Sumatra, Java, and Borneo.
1322–1328: Traveled extensively
inside China.
1328–1330: Set off overland through
Tibet and Persia home to Italy.
See map on page 126

POLO, MARCO
1254–1324   Venice
1271: Left Acre with Nicolò and
Maffeo Polo for Kermān in southeast
Iran, then went south to Hormuz on
Persian Gulf, and returned to Kermān.
Then north to Tunocain and east toward
Harī River, joining the route to China
at Balkh in Afghanistan. Marched
through Hindu Kush and Pamirs to
Oxus River, then down Yaman Yar to
Kashgar and Taklamakan desert. Took
route through desert oases to
Tunhwang.
1275: Reached khan's summer palace at
Shangtu, 180 miles north of Cambaluc.
1275–1292: Traveled within Mongol
Empire—throughout China, to Burma,
Cochin China, and Tonkin.
1292–1295: Traveled back to Venice
via Indochina, Ceylon, India, and Persia.
1298: Captured by Genoese. While in
prison started his *Book*.
See map on page 126

POLO, NICOLÒ
dates unknown   Venice
1255: With his brother Maffeo, sailed
to Constantinople on trading trip.
1260: Sailed on to Sudak in the Crimea,
then went overland to Sarai on the
Volga River.
1262: Went northward from Sarai to
Bolgara, a Mongol camp on the upper
Volga, before continuing southeastward
toward Bukhara (in modern USSR) in an
attempt to make a long detour home.
1265: Joined up with Mongol envoys
to travel to China. Journeyed by way
of Samarkand and the Silk Road to

Tunhwang, then east to the Yellow
River and Cambaluc.
1266: Left Cambaluc on homeward
journey.
1269: Arrived back at Acre in northern
Palestine and embarked for Venice.
1271: Set off again for China, taking his
son Marco.
See map on page 126

RUBRUCK, WILLIAM OF
1215–1270   France
1248: In the retinue of Louis IX of
France, visited the Middle East.
1252–1255: Went to the Great Khan
bearing letters from Louis IX. Started
out from Constantinople on the long
journey to Karakoram and back.
Traveled by sea to Sudak in Crimea then
overland through steppes of central
Asia, by way of Mongol camp on the
River Volga to Karakoram.
See map on page 126

SVARSSON, GARDAR
800's   Sweden
860–870(?): Thought to have been first
Viking to reach Iceland. Driven off
course across the Atlantic from Hebrides
to the southeastern coast of Iceland.
Sailed north to Húsavik, then around
Iceland, proving it an island.
See map on page 53

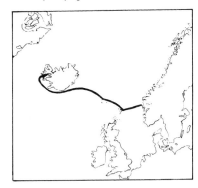

VILGERDASSON, FLOKI
800's   Norway
860–870: First Viking to attempt to settle
in Iceland. Journeyed by way of
Shetlands and Faeroes. Sailed along
south coast of Iceland, then north to
Breidhafjördhur. Gave Iceland its name.

Glossary

allegory: Story which has an underlying meaning different from its surface meaning. Allegories are often used to illustrate moral or religious problems.

asceticism: Manner of life of those who follow the doctrine that rigorous self-denial leads to the attainment of a high level of spirituality and morality. Asceticism also refers to the way of life of people who seek neither pleasure nor comfort.

assassin: A murderer. The name was first given to young Moslems in Persia and Asia Minor in the 1100's. They committed crimes, including murder, for their leader, who gained power over them by use of the drug hashish. *See also Old Man of the Mountain*

brackish: Adjective used to describe the dark cloudy water found in swamps and stagnant pools which is unpleasantly salty in flavor.

caliph: Historically, title of religious and civil leader of Moslem state, e.g. Caliph of Baghdad. The holder of the title was usually elected, but at times it was passed on according to hereditary. The caliph had to be an adult male, sound in mind and body.

caulking: Technique of making an article watertight by sealing seams or joints with a substance such as mud, tar, or glue. Viking ships were caulked with tarred animal hair or wool.

Celts: The early inhabitants of southwestern Germany, parts of the British Isles, and France. They all spoke related dialects of the Indo-European language known as Celtic. Today, forms of the Celtic languages are still spoken in Ireland, the highlands of Scotland, Wales, and Brittany.

coracle: Small, round-bottomed, keelless boat having a wickerwork frame covered with a waterproof layer of animal skin or tarred cloth. Coracles are still made and used by fishermen in Ireland and Wales, and are a great tourist attraction.

corselet: Lightweight armor worn by Vikings and by soldiers in later medieval times to protect the chest and back against injury.

couvade: Practice among certain primitive peoples by which the father takes to his bed after a baby is born, while the mother goes about her usual tasks in the home or fields.

cowrie: A mollusk found in warm seas. Its highly polished shells, often brightly colored, were once used as currency in parts of Asia and Africa.

crosier: Ceremonial stave carried as a badge of office by a bishop.

Crusades: Christian military expeditions undertaken during 1000's, 1100's, and 1200's, in attempts to recover Palestine, the land of Jesus Christ, from the Moslems and to prevent the spread of Islam. The word *crusade* comes from the Latin word for a cross.

Danegeld: Regular tax in medieval England. It was originally levied as tribute to Danish invaders, and later continued for other purposes.

Danelaw: The part of northeastern England, ruled by the Danes from the 800's. It was named for the system of laws enforced there by Danish rulers.

dragon ships: Long, narrow warships, often with a dragon's head carved on the prow. They were used by Vikings for quick surprise raids. Because of their shallow draught, they could be taken inland along rivers. They could be rowed, or sailed with a square woolen sail.

envoy: An accredited messenger or representative.

feudalism: Political and military system in medieval Europe. It was an arrangement between the ruling lords, who owned most of the land, and their vassals or subjects. In exchange for military and domestic services and goods, the lord gave land to his vassals. Lords and vassals took vows of allegiance and obligation to each other. The peasants were protected by their lords from outside attack in return for goods and labor.

Genghis Khan: From Turkic words meaning *chief of all the oceans*. The title was taken by the Mongol ruler Temujin who built up the vast Mongol Empire in the early 1200's.

glacier: Slow-moving mass of ice formed by the accumulation of unmelted snow over the years. There are two kinds of glaciers—*valley glaciers* are river valley masses, *continental glaciers* cover plateaus or whole mountain ranges apart from the highest peaks. The Greenland Icecap, a continental glacier, covers 668,000 square miles, and is the second largest in the world.

Golden Horde: One of the western khanates of the Mongol Empire, comprising southern Russia and Kazakhstan. The Golden Horde was set up by Batu, grandson of Genghis Khan.

Grand Canal: 900-mile long, man-made river, extending from just south of Peking to Hangchow. One of China's most important waterways, it was built by Chinese in the A.D. 600's. They joined existing rivers and lakes with artificial channels. The canal was improved under the Mongol occupation.

Great Wall of China: Longest fortified wall ever built. Originally a series of walls linked together in the 200's , as a defense for China against barbarians. The wall, parts of which still exist, averages 30 feet high with towers 35 or 40 feet high every 200 or 300 yards. The wall was built of brick, earth, and stone.

heretic: Person who maintains religious opinions contrary to those accepted by his church, or rejects doctrines prescribed by his church.

hot spring: Natural spring with water hotter than the surrounding air, especially one above 98°F.

infidel : Generally, a heathen or unbeliever. Historically, Christians referred to Moslems as infidels, and vice versa.

Islands of the Blessed : Legendary islands to the west of the British Isles, thought by classical writers to be a kind of earthly paradise.

knärr : Large, broad-bottomed merchant ship used by Vikings for trading or long-distance voyages, and for carrying large numbers of people.

mirage : An optical phenomenon caused by the refraction (bending) of light rays from the sky toward the viewer's eyes. Refraction occurs as the rays strike the hot air just above the earth's surface. Distant objects appear, often inverted, to be nearer than they are, and the reflection of a cloud in the sky can give the illusion of a lake. Mirages often occur in the desert and can delude thirsty travelers into imagining they are near water.

Nestorians : Members of a heretical Christian sect which believed that there were not only two distinct natures in Christ, the human and the divine, but also two separate persons. Because of this, Nestorians also believed that Mary was not the mother of God. Small groups of the sect were found scattered throughout Asia in medieval times. The sect was most prominent in the A.D. 400's. Nestorius, for whom the sect was named, was a bishop of Constantinople (now Istanbul).

Old Man of the Mountain : Legendary figure based on real-life characters of a line of Moslem pontiffs. According to the legend, the Old Man lived in a castle south of the Caspian Sea. He induced his followers—Assassins—to commit murders through use of the drug hashish.
See also assassin

Ovis poli : Long-horned mountain sheep first observed in the mountains of central Asia by Marco Polo.

pillage : To plunder money and goods by violence or while at war.

Prester John : Legendary Christian potentate supposed by people in the Middle Ages to have ruled over a large kingdom in some remote Asian or African country.

retinue : A body of servants or attendants. The retinue of a medieval king on a journey abroad included noblemen with their own attendants, servants, grooms, chaplains, secretaries, interpreters, musicians, and any number of other persons.

roof of the world : Name given to the high plateau of the Pamirs where the surrounding mountain ranges meet.

saga : Medieval Norse or Icelandic prose narrative, usually concerning the heroic achievements of a person or a family. Sometimes a saga recorded information about a whole community, including the names of all members of each family, their possessions and the place they inhabited. The *Landnamabók* and the *Flateyjarbók* are two very important collections of sagas. Most sagas were collected and written down in the 1200's and 1300's, often by priests.

the seven arts : Seven basic branches of learning on which more advanced studies are founded. In the Middle Ages, the seven were said to be: grammar, logic, rhetoric, arithmetic, geometry, music, and astronomy.

Silk Roads : Trade roads from China to the West, open in the days of the Roman Empire for the transportation of silk to Europe. The Chinese were for centuries the only nation to know the secret of silk making. Use of these roads declined after the fall of Rome. During the days of the Mongol Empire, the roads were opened again for a time to western travelers.

Skraeling : Name given by Vikings to the native inhabitants, Eskimos and American Indians, of the northern

lands in which they settled. No distinction was made by Vikings among the different tribes they must have encountered—they were all *Skraelings*, meaning foreigners.

subsistence farming : Farming on such a small scale that the farmer has no profit or surplus. Such farmers live at the mercy of the weather because they cannot build up emergency stores.

Syra Orda : The summer camp of Genghis Khan, west of Cambaluc, visited by Friar Carpini. The Mongols, even at the height of their empire, remained nomadic in spirit, and seldom stayed long in one place. Twice a year the khan moved his entire court to a different encampment. *Orda*, a word which survives as horde, means camp.

Valkyries : Beautiful warlike goddess maidens in Norse mythology. Odin, the chief god, sent them to collect dead heroes from the battlefield for Valhalla, the hall of dead heroes.

Vinland : Name given to the land discovered by the Viking Leif, son of Eric the Red. Its exact position cannot be proved, but it is thought to be on the North American coast between Newfoundland and Long Island.

yellow peril : the supposed danger to Western civilization from the growth of power and influence of the peoples of China and Japan.

Index

Picture Credits

Listed below are the sources of all the illustrations in this book. To identify the source of a particular illustration, first find the relevant page on the diagram opposite. The number in black in the appropriate position on that page refers to the credit as listed below.

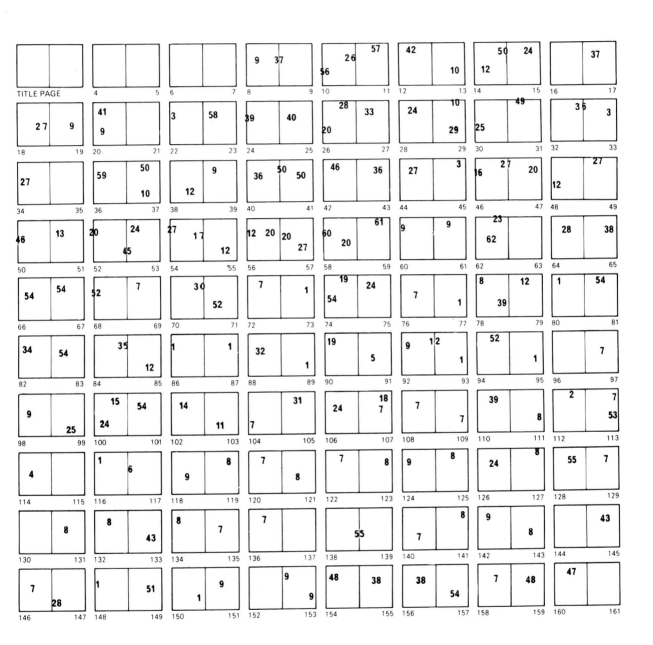